DELIGHTFUL THREE MINUTE OBJECT-LESSONS

by

JOHN HENRY SARGENT

BAKER BOOK HOUSE
Grand Rapids, Michigan

PHOTOLITHOPRINTED BY CUSHING - MALLOY, INC.
ANN ARBOR, MICHIGAN, UNITED STATES OF AMERICA
1 9 7 3

FOREWORD

I have read the list of seventy odd parables, and am thrilled. You have the same genius for taking common things and weaving them into a delightful and inspiring parable, that made Jesus so forceful. I know you learned your art by memorizing and living His parables.

We are planning to use a great many of your parables for translation into other languages for our students. They have a universality of appeal which takes them to every land and to every home.

Our committee is hunting high and low for enough good fascinating reading that can be written in the language of every continent. Very very little has proven adaptable. Nearly all that we investigate loses its poignancy when transplanted to other shores. But you deal with the things that are found everywhere: bridges, colored ribbons, hinges, lamps, matches, perfumes, pumps, shadows, a growing tree, whistles, cold water, a running brook.

Keep on enriching the literature of children and mothers, and teachers, and my illiterates all over the world.

God bless you.

FRANK C. LAUBACH

CONTENTS
ALPHABETICALLY ARRANGED

ANTENNAS

As you walk along our streets, or ride with your parents out in the country you will notice that on the roofs of many of the houses you pass there are some wire-like pieces of metal upheld in a vertical or horizontal position by an upright rod. The dictionary says this "aerial wire is for the purpose of transmitting or receiving electric waves in wireless telegraphy."

When you see these antennas you often say: "They have a television set in that house."

It is more difficult to transmit vision waves to a distant place because they travel in a straight line and when they strike a mountain or high hill they stop! So at that point there has to be a "relay" which will take the waves and start them going again! Soon those vision waves pass along the area where you live and the antenna on the roof of your house—or on top of the television set,—catches them and transmits them into the mechanism of your set and you see the picture on the screen.

God made antennas long before man did. Those "feelers" on the heads of some insects and snails are antennas for their protection. By them they "feel" or "see" any danger that might be near them in time to run and hide.

An antenna is the means by which messages are transmitted from one place to another. When Jesus came to give God's message of love and power to the world He chose disciples and told them to "go preach,"—to relay God's word into people's homes in distant lands.

I sincerely trust that your thoughts and faith are high enough to catch the message of God's love and the vision of Jesus, and that by your life you relay it to many many other young folks. Like the antenna,—receive and deliver.

"Go ye into all the world and preach the gospel to every creature."—MARK 16:15.

A PRAYER

DEAR God, our Father, help us catch the meaning of thy loving message as expressed in the life of Jesus. Use us as messengers to relay thy gospel truth to young folks who have not learned of thee.

Please, dear Lord, show us ways whereby we may help cause thy kindness and love to be in every human heart, that hate and jealousy may be no more, and that peace may come to the whole world.

Teach us to pray that we may receive thy words of counsel, and give us strength and the desire to pass them along to others.

Bless our homes and our churches, that through them, thy love may encrease in us, as it was lived in Jesus our Lord. Amen.

A MESSAGE FROM OUR BIBLE

"And he said unto them, Go ye into all the world, and preach the gospel to every creature.

He that believeth and is baptized shall be saved; but he that believeth not shall be condemned.

And they went forth, and preached every where, the Lord working with them, and confirming the word with signs following."—MARK 16:15–16, 20.

2

APPROACHING TUNNELS

HAVE you ever sat in a car toward the rear of a train and in going around a curve in the road watch the engine puffing and steaming as it pulled you closer and closer to a very small hole in the side of a high mountain?

Of course you know that hole in the mountain is big enough to let the train through all right for it's a railroad tunnel made for that purpose but it looks far too small.

However, you feel safe so you don't scream and jump off, or pull the "Stop" signal valve! You just watch with fascination as that seemingly approaching tunnel grows bigger and bigger. The train straightens out and you lose sight of the engine but suddenly you are inside the tunnel and sure enough there is plenty of room on both sides of the train, and above it. You are safe.

Now, of course, the tunnel didn't grow any bigger, nor did the train shrink any in size—it was your vision that changed.

As you approached the tunnel it began to reveal itself in the true size—you saw it in its right proportion,—it began to prove itself adequate to your need. And when you finally reached it, it safely surrounded you and gave you safe passage.

It seems to me that your relationship to God is something like that. It may often seem to you that he is far away and that your problem won't be noticed or considered by him. You know God exists but he seems so far off. My young friends, prayer is the vehicle that carries you nearer and nearer to him. By prayer you approach God and as you draw nearer to him you see him in larger vision—in greater proportion—you see him as he is, until his all-surrounding love has done away with your fear and you are safe and happy.

" . . . As he drew near . . . the voice of the Lord came unto him."—THE ACTS 7:31.

[13]

A PRAYER

GRANT, O God, that we may draw nearer unto thee each day. Give us clear vision that we may be aware of the greatness and gentleness of thy love.

Help us have a great faith that in all our earthly problems we may see the bigness of thy kingdom.

Draw us more closely to thyself that thy love and kindness may be revealed to us in all its goodness and power, to guide us in our ways of living.

Comfort those who are distressed in mind and attitude. Restore health and strength to the sick and the weak.

Bless those who care for them and give them peace of mind by thy spirit.

Watch over our homes and may love and peace come to the world and prevail among men of all nations, and teach us the truth and righteousness of Jesus Christ our Lord. Amen.

A MESSAGE FROM OUR BIBLE

"And when forty years were expired, there appeared to him in the wilderness of mount Sina an angel of the Lord in a flame of fire in a bush.

When Moses saw it, he wondered at the sight; and as he drew near to behold it, the voice of the Lord came unto him.

I am God of thy fathers,—Then Moses trembled, and durst not behold.

Then said the Lord to him, Put off thy shoes from thy feet; for the place where thou standest is holy ground." THE ACTS 7:30–33.

ATOMIZERS

In large apple orchards the farmer goes among the trees with a spraying machine. In the tank there is some liquid, and compressed air forces it out of a tiny hole or nozzle and it appears as a spray so that all the apple buds on one tree receive it at the same time.

It's a kind of Atomizer which, perhaps you have used when you had a sore throat, in order to kill those tiny germs that collected there.

The dictionary says about "Atomizers": "Liquids in the form of spray are said to be pulverized,—or atomized." "Reduced to atoms." So you see, a little liquid is turned into a lot of spray by the Atomizer, and a few drops cover a large area, and because those trees were sprayed you can buy lovely, smooth, juicy, red apples; and nice green apples for that pie.

You know, boys and girls, it seems to me that Christianity is spread that way by all of us who truly love God. Let us take Jesus as an example,—he possessed in his heart, the love of God his Father and by his many many acts of kindness and deeds of mercy, and words of wisdom, he spread it to hundreds of people and even thousands and millions, for indeed, after nearly 2000 years, it still is reaching people's hearts in increasing numbers through his helpers.

God wants you to be one of those helpers who will always live a Christian life and every day you can influence many other children to be more like Jesus. Like the atomizer you spread your life to many who need you to make them happy.

"Let him who is taught in the word, communicate . . ."—GALATIANS 6:6.

A PRAYER

DEAR Lord, our God, for thy great goodness towards us, we thank thee. When sorrow and strife have disturbed us, thy strength and guidance have given us courage and understanding.

Direct us as a church, O God, and as a nation. Cause us to see clearly the way of peace on earth.

Give wisdom to all our leaders and help each one to do the work that is set before him, and give to all a true sense of values.

Bless the children and their parents and may they find their strength in Jesus Christ, our Saviour. Amen.

A MESSAGE FROM OUR BIBLE

"Let him that is taught in the word communicate unto him that teacheth in all good things.

And let us not be weary in well doing; for in due season we shall reap, if we faint not.

As we have therefore opportunity, let us do good unto all, especially unto them who are of the household of faith."—GALATIANS 6 :6, 9–10.

BLUEPRINTS

WHEN you and your mother go to the store to buy a pattern for a new dress you look for the picture on the envelope that best suits your taste. Then you go home and spread the pattern on the table and cut the cloth to match the various pieces of the blueprint. You see, the pattern is a kind of blueprint of what the dress is to look like.

When your father decides to build a house or a shop or garage he goes to an architect who shows him pictures of houses, or whatever he wants to have built, and when he has decided on a certain style the architect draws the plan on sensitized paper, which, when exposed to the bright light becomes the blueprint or likeness of the building your father has selected.

The carpenters can then go to work and build it like the architect's pattern—or blueprint.

When the Indians possessed this country they would talk to each other by the use of signs—a stone in a certain position meant something to the person who might be following. Three stones meant something else. Bent twigs and smoke signals had their meaning—not strictly blueprints—yet they were patterns, outlining certain messages.

Recipes might be called blueprints especially when the words are pictured instead of written—as for "one spoonful,"—a spoon is drawn. This makes it easy for a child to follow and to put the right ingredients together and produce a cake.

The Bible tells us that God made us in his own image and because we do not see God, he sent Jesus to us that we might make our lives like him, building our character, according to his example, conducting ourselves after the pattern set for us by his way of life.

"Jesus shall change our body that it may be fashioned like unto his glorious body."—PHILIPPIANS 3:21.

A PRAYER

DEAR God, we thank thee for singing birds, for beautiful flowers, for the fruit of trees, for the green grass and the rain and snow.

Help us, O God, to be of use and grant that our cheerfulness may bring a bit of joy to someone who is discouraged, that our kindness may help lift another's burden, that our prayers will touch the hearts of many and turn them toward thee.

Lead us, we pray, to greater beauty in thy world, and strengthen us with thy spirit that we may bring peace and brotherhood among the nations.   Amen.

A MESSAGE FROM OUR BIBLE

"Let us therefore, as many as be perfect, be thus minded; and if in any thing ye be otherwise minded, God shall reveal even this unto you.

Nevertheless, whereto we have already attained, let us walk by the same rule, let us mind the same thing.

For our conversation is in heaven; from whence also we look for the Saviour, the Lord Jesus Christ;

Who shall change our vile body, that it may be fashioned like unto his glorious body, according to the working whereby he is able even to subdue all things unto himself."—PHILIPPIANS 3:15–16, 20–21.

BRIDGES

I'LL bet many of you have had the experience I had once when out fishing in a trout brook. I wanted to cross over to the other side,—so, seeing stones in the stream I thought I could easily step from one to another and get over all right. But I slipped—and went home, very wet! Most bridges have protecting handrails but this stepping-stone bridge didn't!

You see there are many kinds of bridges. A tree fallen across a stream is a bridge. Then there is Brooklyn Bridge,—and the Golden Gate Bridge.

Once I crossed over a rather rickety bridge when there was a flood raging. Less than two hours later, the bridge washed away. It made it very difficult in getting back over the river again. You see bridges work both ways—like a cross-cut saw.

Words are bridges. They carry messages from one person to another.

Your school books are bridges and as you go along through the pages of these books, day after day, you are traveling over a sea of ignorance to knowledge; over creeks to new truths.

And then, I think of prayer as a bridge—a bridge to God. By prayer we go to him and tell him our troubles and he brings to us his blessing. We go to him with our joys and he rejoices with us, as he comes into our homes. We recall the story of Jacob's ladder reaching up to God, —I like to think of prayer as a way, a bridge, by which means God and I are often brought together.

We talk to God by way of prayer and if we don't destroy the bridge—if I just wait and listen—he will reveal to me his counsel.

"... *effectual, fervent prayer of a righteous man availeth much."*—JAMES 5 :16.

A PRAYER

Our Father, we would honor thee today, and be reverent before thee. Thy presence is real in our hearts and we rejoice that thou dost care for us, and encourage us in all our undertakings.

Create in us clean minds, that we may think clearly and so find wisdom by which we may make a better world.

Help the young people of our church and community to understand the needs of this generation, and give us strength to follow after the pattern of Jesus.

Bless our homes, dear God, and give us wisdom to know right from wrong, and the spiritual strength and inclination to choose rightly in order that we may be a part in building that better world in peace and in Christian fellowship. Amen.

A Message from Our Bible

"Above all things swear not, neither by heaven, neither by earth, neither by any other oath; but let your yea be yea; and your nay, nay; lest ye fall into condemnation.

Is any among you afflicted? let him pray. Is any merry? let him sing psalms.

The prayer of faith shall save the sick, and the Lord shall raise him up; and if ye have committed sins, they shall be forgiven him.

Confess your faults one to another, and pray one for another, that ye may be healed. The effectual fervent prayer of a righteous man availeth much."—James 5:12–13, 15–16.

6

CHAINS

DURING the cold winter months when the New England country roads are often snowy and slippery because of icy places, chains are often attached to the rear wheels of automobiles for the sake of safety.

After the chains have been used awhile there comes a familiar sound—wham, bang, bang! A link in the chain has broken and it ceases to be as useful as a protective chain.

Isn't that the way with God's Church? When someone allows his enthusiasm for God's work to wear out, the church is weakened, and it becomes more difficult to carry along Christ's program.

We often think of chains as bad habits—like criminals on a chain gang—to hold them back.

Such bad-habit chains keep us from being free to do what ought to be done. Our work suffers. Bad habits keep us from doing, or being, our best. Let's not be chained to or by bad habits.

If I should ask you what is held in the right hand of the lady Statue of Liberty you could doubtless tell me. It's a torch, representing a light. This signifies that all who come to America are assured of freedom as revealed and promised in the book she holds in her left hand: "The Declaration of Independence" and all this is proved by the fact that the bonds of tyranny will here be shaken off forever as shown by what lies at her feet . . . a broken chain.

It is indeed, the truth, that if you will hold high the Light of God's love, and live so as to point to His law as revealed in Jesus and his Gospel; the chains that tend to bind us to untruth and injustice and evil habits will be broken, and we will always be free to serve Christ and so find peace.

____

"And the chains fell off his hands."—ACTS 12:7.

A PRAYER

Dear God, our Father, help us keep our minds free from all prejudices. Make us friendly toward all people. Keep us from evil ways and wrong ideas that we may be free to rightfully serve thee.

Grant that in our hearts will live the love as it was lived by Jesus.

Help those who are in trouble, whose consciences are disturbing them. Give them the spiritual strength they need to right all wrongs and cease doing evil.

Bless the children of all lands,—especially those in devastated areas—where food is scarce and clothes are wanting.

Stir us all into action for giving that they may be supplied with food and protection. Thus we seek thy strength, dear Lord, for our endeavors. Amen.

A Message from Our Bible

"And behold the angel of the Lord came upon him and a light shined in the prison: and he smote Peter on the side, and raised him up, saying, Arise up quickly. And his chains fell off from his hands.

And the angel said unto him, Gird thyself, and bind on thy sandals; and so he did. And he saith unto him, Cast thy garments about thee, and follow me.

And he went out, and followed him; and wist not that it was true which was done by the angel; but thought he saw a vision."—Acts 12:7, 8, 9.

CHALK

CHALK is hard earth,—or soft white rock. It is formed under water by the disintegration of tiny shells and little animals, seaweed, coral, fishes and small reptiles. These dead things accumulate, and by natural chemical processes form this white lime substance on the bottom of the ocean.

In the process of millions of centuries, this ocean bed becomes dry land. An example of this is the promontory known as the white cliffs of Dover.

We know chalk best through its use as a crayon.

Sometimes at recess in school you have the urge to draw a picture, a dog, or a donkey or your pal, so you find a piece of chalk and go to work. If you have different colored chalk then you think you are quite an artist but the piece of chalk grows smaller and smaller as you leave part of it on the chalkboard. Then you write under it "this is a cat"—or whatever you intended it to be—and a bit of chalk is left to show others what you have written.

Every day you go to school or church or up town you leave a mark on the people who notice you.

Are you friendly? Do you smile to the people you know when they speak—or do you turn away? Are you grouchy and thoughtless? Do you and your gang take up all the sidewalk and push old people into the street? Or are you courteous?

What is the mark of your language as you pass by? What kind of impression do you make at school or church? Would people be glad or sorry to have you move to another State?

We all leave a bit of ourselves when we pass by. Is that mark clean and white and will people be better and happier because of you?

"I bear in my body the marks of the Lord."—GALA-TIANS 6:17.

A PRAYER

Our Father God, help us to so live day by day that we may truly be a help in the perfecting of thy plan for our world.

Use us, dear Lord, as we work and as we play—at home, at school or in factory or office. Grant that our lives may count for thee and thy way of life through Jesus Christ.

Give us peace, O God; destroy the causes of unrest and bitterness. Help all who are troubled, who need the kindness of Christian friends, and give us an understanding mind and heart to leave with them a more cheerful outlook.

Direct our ways to the end that Christian love may order the peace of the world. Amen.

A Message from Our Bible

"Bear ye one another's burdens, and so fulfil the law of Christ.

For if a man think himself to be something, when he is nothing, he deceiveth himself.

But let every man prove his own work, and then shall he have rejoicing in himself alone, and not in another.

For every man shall bear his own burden.

Let him that is taught in the word communicate unto him that teacheth in all good things."—Galatians 6:2–6.

CLOCKS

THINKING back to several years ago when I was a boy I remember how my father, after the chores were all done and supper was out of the way and the Bible had been read, every Saturday night, used to wind the big eight-day clock. That clock would run perfectly and keep good time for seven days. The eighth day it would begin to lose time!

Once every year or two a spring inside that clock would break and strangely enough it would happen usually on a Friday or Saturday. It would seem that clock springs break easier and more frequently when they are nearly run down! Well, so do we!

Have you ever noticed that when you are up too late at night and you are very tired the next morning,—you are inclined to be irritable, and sometimes downright cross and hateful?

You see, just as that clock needed someone to wind it, —to keep it strong and working right, so you need strengthening every day and especially on Sundays by the love of God, allowing His spiritual power to energize you.

Then I thought of the electric clocks. They never seem to stop or run down. They just go on and on without breaking, giving us the right time—all because the power is constantly going into them—every day—every hour, minute by minute.

Like the clock, I'm sure we all would be better people —better natured, and be much more worth while, if we would pay more attention to God, asking Him to pour His strength into us; also let us read the Bible every day that we may be filled with the wise counsel Jesus so dearly gave as recorded in the Gospels for, you know,—

"They that wait upon the Lord shall renew their strength."—ISAIAH 40:31.

A PRAYER

Dear God, our Father, we pray thee in acknowledgment of thy great goodness and love in the world.

We do appreciate the many opportunities available to us whereby we may serve thy plan of peace for the world. Keep us faithful and dependable, that thy way of Christian love may spread through our efforts.

May we have the enthusiasm to establish Christianity in our community and nation as we have for our own pleasures and interests. Help us as we worship and work, to make the church prominent in our every day life, and mold our lives in the likeness of Jesus. Amen.

A Message from Our Bible

"The everlasting God, the Lord, the Creator of the ends of the earth, fainteth not neither is weary; there is no searching of his understanding.

He giveth power to the faint and to him that hath no might he increaseth strength.

Even the youths shall faint and be weary, and the young men shall utterly fall;

But they that wait for the Lord shall renew their strength; they shall mount up with wings as eagles; they shall run, and not be weary; they shall walk, and not faint."—Isaiah 40:28–31.

9
COLOR

I WONDER if you children who live in the city have all seen a rainbow. All those beautiful colors you see are caused by the sun shining through the rain. You can get the same colors at a waterfall or even by emptying a pan of water in the bright sunlight.

All children love colorful things because they are prettier than black. Colors are cheerful. When mother takes you to buy a dress, you ask for yellow or red or pink or perhaps blue. A boy doesn't buy a black tie,—neither do I!

God knew we would all love color, so He made the flowers grow. He never made a black carnation—I never saw a black rose!

In the hills of New Hampshire the mountain sides are ablaze with beauty because of the leaves of the trees. Some are red, some yellow, others are brown—all blending together with the green.

This summer, along the North Shore on Cape Ann, I had occasion to watch artists painting. They seemed to see color in everything, even where I could see no color. It seems strange to me how an artist can dip his brush in red and blue and it comes out violet; or white and red and it comes out pink; or black and yellow and red and he gets brown; and blue and yellow makes green.

Beauty is a combination of colors blending together— like the rainbow—the mountain side—the finished picture.

God meant the world to be like that—beautiful—made so by people of every race and color, living and working and playing together happily and in harmony. The touch of Christianity on any life, beautifies it.

"He made him a coat of many colors."—GENESIS 37:3.

A PRAYER

We thank thee, O God, for the beauty in this world. We find it on every hand,—on the hills, in the valley—the streams and the deserts, the blue sky and the green grass.

We pray that the character of our lives be sincere, the deeds we do be kind, that our thoughts be right.

Make us worthy of being thy children, dear Lord, and bless our homes and teach us thy love, that we may apply it in our everyday living, through Jesus Christ our Lord. Amen.

A Message from Our Bible

"O sing unto the Lord a new song; sing unto the Lord; all the earth.

Sing unto the Lord, bless his name; show forth his salvation from day to day.

Declare his glory among the heathen, his wonders among all peoples.

For the Lord is great, and greatly to be praised; he is to be feared above all gods.

For all the gods of the nations are idols; but the Lord made the heavens.

Honor and majesty are before him; strength and beauty are in his sanctuary.

O worship the Lord in the beauty of holiness; fear before him all the earth."—Psalm 96:1–6, 9.

COLORED RIBBONS

DURING these few days just before Christmas there is a certain secrecy in the air. Packages are being received from the mailman and immediately whisked to the attic or some closet or high on a shelf. The outside wrapping is taken off and there, revealed, are many small packages carefully covered with Christmas paper and surrounded with all colors of ribbons—white, red, brown, yellow, green—and in one corner of the package, sure enough, there is that notice "Do not open until Christmas."

So you just look at the beautiful packages with their lovely colored ribbons—and wonder expectantly, what might be inside. You know there will be nice gifts and useful ones, worthy of the giver and of you. A lot of love is wrapped under those colored ribbons.

God has given us this world in beautifully colored wrappings and ribbons. Flowers are all around us. Beautifully colored birds. The trees on the hillsides are many colors blended into loveliness with the green foliage and grass. Man even uses paint to adorn his house because of his great pride in the knowledge that he has established a home inside.

Even man himself, God has made of different hue. White, brown, reddish, yellow and even black.

Wrapped up inside these ribbons of various colors God has placed His love. The whole world of nature and of people is full of God's love.

God wants every day to be Christmas Day, his day, for all his children.

Let us all try, at home and at school and on the street, to see the beautiful in life around us and know that underneath, and within, God's love fills the earth with joy and peace.

"The earth is the Lord's and the fulness there of."— PSALM 24:1.

A PRAYER

FORGIVE us, dear Lord, if at Christmas time we seem to be a bit selfish. Beautifully colored packages attract our attention and we are anxious to know their contents. Grant that all children, everywhere, may have the Christmas spirit and that all may receive a gift. More important than all else is that thy love will touch the hearts of all people in the whole world and cause everyone to find peace and happiness in one's self, and a desire to freely give as Jesus did. Amen.

THE MESSAGE FROM OUR BIBLE

"The earth is the Lord's, and the fulness thereof. The world and they that dwell therein.

For he hath founded it upon the seas, And established it upon the floods.

Who shall ascend into the hill of the Lord? And who shall stand in his holy place?

He that hath clean hands, and a pure heart; Who hath not lifted up his soul unto falsehood, And hath not sworn deceitfully.

He shall receive a blessing from the Lord, and righteousness from the God of his salvation."—PSALM 24:1–5.

COOKIES

OF COURSE every girl knows how to cook, and I think every boy, also, should learn how to put ingredients together in such a way that they will come out "cookies" or "doughnuts" or even "a pie." Oh I know that Boy Scouts can go on a hike and build a fire without matches and boil and bake potatoes and cook flapjacks and hamburgers! But that's easy.

Then there are these prepared mixtures and all you have to do is put water or milk with them and out comes a cake. That's not enough to know!

Imagine making an automobile that way—or a house—just buying a bag of powered iron, wood and upholstery, mix it with water and out comes a Pontiac or a Ford depending on what label is on the bag of powder.

Wouldn't it be nice if you could get your home work done that way?

You'll be surprised at how many ingredients go into the making of a good batch of cookies. Go ask your mother about it! She'll give you a recipe with all the instructions for using the ingredients called for.

God made this world to be a lovely garden. He gave us the recipe for making it so, but so many have failed to follow the instructions Jesus has given, that weeds of hatred and greed and evil have spoiled the garden. How easy it is to burn the cookies after they are all made!

You see you boys and girls are the ingredients that make this world,—God's garden—boys and girls of different races and color and ideas—and if you will all follow the teachings of Jesus and the other Bible truths,—God's recipe—and keep yourself from getting "burned" by wrong-doing and selfish acts you can make this world as God wants it to be,—beautiful, and useful and peaceful.

"I am the way, the truth and the life."—JOHN 14:6.

A PRAYER

Dear Lord, use us each day in such a way that will cause our homes and our schools to be more and more worthy of thy love and plan.

Help us as a family to work and play together, that our home will grow in happiness, and teach us to be generous, for, in sharing the things we have with others will make for cheer and happiness and peace around us and reach out to the whole world.

So help us to be more like thee as thou didst give thyself without thought of rewards. Amen.

Words of Jesus in Our Bible

"Let not your heart be troubled; ye believe in God believe also in me.

In my Father's house are many mansions; if it were not so, I would have told you. I go to prepare a place for you.

And if I go and prepare a place for you, I will come again, and receive you unto myself; there where I am, there ye may be also.

And whither I go ye know, and the way ye know.

Jesus saith unto him (Thomas), I am the way, the truth, and the life; no man cometh unto the Father, but by me."—JOHN 14:1–4, 6.

CRACKS

Some time ago I stood on the edge of the Grand Canyon. Although it was only one mile across from rim to rim, one would have to travel nearly two hundred miles to reach the opposite point. The Canyon is one mile deep and reminded me of being a great crack in the earth's surface. Actually, of course, it was formed by the Colorado River.

Indeed, off the Aleutian Islands, and near Japan, there are two great cracks in the ocean floor caused by earthquakes, making the depth of the ocean, at that point, over 6 miles!

On the outside of one of the parsonages in which I lived there was a large fireplace chimney, and one day, after an earthquake had been felt, I noticed a crack in that chimney which I could follow, with my eyes, from the ground to the very top. You see the foundation of our house settled at one corner, just enough to cause that break all the way up the chimney. That crack is a symptom—a result of something wrong at the foundation.

When the doctor calls and he sees that you have a swelling on your neck or a rash on your chest he takes your temperature and says you have the mumps,—or the measles! All he sees is the symptoms—like the crack in the chimney—and he knows what the disease is that causes it,—something is wrong inside, and outside appearances tell us what it is. They are the "evidences of things not seen."

So it is when a person acts wickedly or says vulgar words and swears—we know, by these symptoms, that his heart isn't quite right with God—there is something wrong inside of him and like the crack, the evidences, or symptoms are shown in his actions and words.

"Like a man that built a house without a foundation."
—Luke 6:49.

A PRAYER

O GOD, our Father, we thank thee for our homes and for our friends and the love thou dost have for us all. Give us the wisdom to know the right and to always speak the truth. Grant that the inspiration of thy goodness may make us good; that thy teaching of thoughtfulness may make us kind.

Keep us faithful, dear Lord, and help us to deserve thy love that we may apply it toward one another and so have peace on the earth. Teach us to worship and help all young folks to pray. Amen.

THE MESSAGE FROM OUR BIBLE

"Whosoever cometh to me, and heareth my sayings, and doeth them, I will show you to whom he is like:

He is like a man who built a house, and digged deep, and laid the foundation on a rock; and when the flood arose, the stream beat vehemently upon that house, and could not shake it; for it was founded upon a rock."— LUKE 6:47–48.

DIAMONDS

A LONG long time ago a colored man in Africa was walking along a beach and the mud flats of his native land and suddenly saw a brilliant stone fairly sparkling in the sunlight. Now he had walked that way before but all he saw was mud and sand.

He picked up this stone and after a while swapped it for some small trinket a white trader had in his possession who, in turn, sold it for a huge some of money! Yes, it was a diamond, and today that field is protected by a very large police force.

A few years ago a tiny bit of radium was lost, purposely taken from its locker, or just misplaced. People looked everywhere for it,—all over the hospital and grounds, and then someone thought of a finder. This finder works the way a finder for buried mines does on a battlefield. If the radium was found it was because it stood out so prominently before the searching "eyes" of that finder.

When Jesus walked this earth people had no trouble picking him out in a crowd or market place. Wherever he was he shined forth in the multitude and people rushed to be near him. Whenever he spoke people listened, for his council was always good.

When you are walking along the street do you suppose the people you meet recognize you as a Christian? Or are you careless of your actions and thoughtless of what you say?

As the sparking diamond stood out among the grains of sand,—so Jesus gave light and joy to the whole world —will you make that Christian light yours and spread brightness along your way in school and home.

"I am come a light into the world . . ."—JOHN 12:46.

A PRAYER

Dear God, our Father, thou art our most precious possession; help us to never lose sight of thee.

We know thou art with us wherever we are, but sometimes we turn away from thee and do things that are wrong. We often say words that hurt others,—help us to stop and think, before we speak, and in so doing we shall see thee; and thy presence will guide us.

Bless our homes, dear Lord, and help us see thee there each day to guide and counsel us. Amen.

A Message from Our Bible

"Jesus said, He that believeth on me, believeth on him that sent me.

And he that seeth me seeth him that sent me.

I am come a light into the world, that whosoever believeth on me should not abide in darkness.

And if any man hear my words, and believe not, I judge him not; For I come not to judge the world, but to save the world.

I have not spoken of myself; but the Father which sent me, he gave me a commandment, what I should say, and what I should speak."—John 12:44–47, 49.

"DOOR-STONES"

As YOU go through the Arcade of Plymouth Church of the Pilgrims in Brooklyn, New York, you see a stone under which are these words, "Piece of Plymouth Rock given 'Church of the Pilgrims' about 1840. Placed here Dec. 1940. The Door-Stone of American Liberty."

Several years ago I visited in Plymouth, Massachusetts, and made a tour of the many interesting places, and of course, Plymouth Rock was the outstanding monument to see.

Of course that Rock is fenced in and guarded so that people will not keep chipping souvenirs from it! As I left the Rock and looked out to sea and stood on the shore sands I could not help but think how, over three hundred thirty years ago, our Pilgrim Forefathers stepped from their boat on that Rock and walked up the sandy beach to dry land.

Since then, the Rock, not the sandy beach, has been the symbol of the strength of America. The sands of 1620 have long since disappeared. The sea water has washed up and the tides have dragged them out and replaced them with other sand.

But the rock is still there. Strong,—a symbol of security,—Rooted in a solid foundation, bespeaking fidelity.

Our homes are like that to us—places of security in the strength of the love upon which they are built, the faithfulness of each one of its members to the others.

As Plymouth Rock was the "Door-Stone" of that little boat load of Pilgrims to a new land, in their search for freedom and security in the building of their new homes —so our homes today tell us what America will be tomorrow.

"I am the way, the truth, and the life?"—JOHN 14:6.

A PRAYER

Dear God, our Father, we thank thee for thy Son Jesus who taught us the way to a better life. Each day can be better than the last if we try to find opportunities to bring cheer to someone.

Help us to be happy in our attitude wherever we are —cheerful around our home, and keep us faithful and trustworthy, and lead us by thy spirit of love as thou hast taught us through Jesus Christ our Lord. Amen.

A Message from Our Bible

"Jesus said, I am the way, the truth, and the life; no man cometh unto the Father, but by me.

And whatsoever ye shall ask in my name, that will I do, that the Father may be glorified in the Son.

If ye love me, keep my commandments.

And I will pray the Father, and he shall give you another Comforter, that he may abide with you forever;"—John 14:6, 13–16.

ECLIPSE

WHEN you go home from school and turn on your radio to listen to your favorite program you settle yourself in an easy chair or on the floor for a pleasant half hour.

How disappointed you are sometimes, when a noise comes in between you and the music, or the ball game, or a play which you are anxious to follow, and blocks it off, so that you can't hear a word!

When some boys or girls go to the movies it would seem that their main reason is to comment, either about the picture or about something that happened in school that afternoon, and then laugh—never once thinking of the people near them who want to hear the program.

Good things are often eclipsed by thoughtlessness, by bad things, by evil.

Several times, during your life span, you will see an eclipse of the sun when the little moon steps in between the earth and the sun and darkness comes in your part of our continent.

Many, many years ago people used to be frightened when an eclipse occurred, but gradually everybody came to know that in a short few minutes the light would come again.

In your daily contacts with people, you will find there are influences that get between you and what you know to be right. But if you have faith and if you will pray to God for strength to withstand temptations, light will surely come and happiness will be yours again.

When Jesus was crucified it was dark for a while but his confident assurance of his Father's care and love brought light and joy to a sad world on the third day. Because of Jesus' great trust and faith we call that day Good Friday.

"He that doeth truth cometh to the light."—JOHN 3:21.

A PRAYER

Our Father in Heaven, we thank thee for sonship—for the heritage of thy love which alone can dispel hatreds. For the knowledge of thy truth which can restore confidence in one another. For the giving of thy Son Jesus Christ, whose presence brought peace and whose spirit and teaching will bring brotherhood and confidence and peace on earth among the people of all nations.

We thank thee for Jesus whose strong faith and assurance in thy everlasting power and presence has given us today, a real sure hope that tomorrow the light of thy love and truth will spread over all the earth. Amen.

A Message from Our Bible

"For God so loved the world, that he gave his only begotten Son, that whosoever believeth in him should not perish, but have everlasting life.

For God sent not his Son into the world to condemn the world; but that the world through him might be saved.

For every one that doeth evil hateth the light, neither cometh to the light, lest his deeds should be reproved.

But he that doeth truth cometh to the light, that his deeds may be made manifest, that they are wrought in God."—John 3:16–17, 20–21.

EGGS

DID you ever hear your mother or father say "this old world seems to be upside down"? War takes so many young men away from home. Food prices are so high, as well as everything else. The newspapers are full of stories of wrong-doing. Even young folks become disgruntled sometimes and everything seems to be topsy-turvy,—upside down.

God meant to have happiness and rightness in this world, he wants you to help keep the world right side up.

It's interesting how God makes things. Things that we can't control or change seem to stay right side up,—gravity always acts the right way unless we interfere.

Even an egg is a good example. Of course, you can turn an egg over, but if you do it as fast as you can, the yolk inside never turns over. It is always right side up.

Another interesting fact about eggs is that when you buy a dozen all packed in a carton at the store they are all right end up. How can one tell when an egg is right end up? The small end of the egg should always be down, because there is, in the large end, a bubble of air, and if that end of the egg is kept down too long the air will seep upward and pass through the yellow yolk stirring it up just enough to cause the egg to spoil sooner than it normally would.

In thinking about an egg being right side up in order to keep it fresh and good, I thought how true it is that all of us should endeavor to keep the more important ideas and ideals uppermost in our lives and in our thinking.

Let us never forget to pray, for if we do, life often gets all mixed up and muddled,—upside down. Prayer and thoughts of God give us the life that keep us, and the world, right side up.

"*. . . fervent prayer . . . availeth much.*"—JAMES 5:16.

A PRAYER

DEAR Christ, our Saviour, please remember those who are sick. Make them well if it is thy will. Help all young folks who do not understand thy love and who have never learned of thee. Give us a steady faith that will keep us on the right side of every question, and a will that will cause us to act uprightly, as thou would'st have us do. Amen.

A MESSAGE FROM OUR BIBLE

"Is any among you afflicted? Let him pray. Is any merry? let him sing psalms.

And the prayer of faith shall save the sick, and the Lord shall raise him up; and if he have committed sins, they shall be forgiven him.

Confess your faults one to another, and pray one for another, that ye may be healed. The effectual fervent prayer of a righteous man availeth much."—JAMES 5:13, 15–16.

EMBLEMS

ONE of the most beautiful sights is an American Flag flying in the breeze. Its red, white and blue colors remind us that we want our country to be strong, clean and noble; for it waves as an Emblem of America.

An Emblem seeks to describe the object it represents, as the emblem of the Cross represents Christianity, reminding us that Jesus died on a Cross.

White is emblematic of royalty, because it denotes truth and purity. Kings and Judges wear robes of white ermine fur, signifying honest judgment and purety of thinking.

I read a story once about the method used in catching that little animal the Ermine. He is one of the most beautiful of animals and so clean.

The Ermine lives in the extreme cold regions of Norway, Sweden and Canada, finding shelter in caves and hollow trees.

It is extremely expensive because it is most difficult to catch. As guns or traps cannot be used, the hunter trains his dog to catch the Ermine without biting it and so spoiling its silky fur.

To find this tiny creature the hunter first looks for the cave or tree where he lives, and then he strews mud and dirt all around the entrance and waits!

When the Ermine comes home he sees the repulsive dirt and thinks of his beautiful fur as the emblem of purity, and refuses to enter his shelter for fear of soiling that white loveliness.

Rather than enter an unclean place he faces the yelping dogs. He has only a white coat, but he gives his life to keep it clean and pure.

"Blessed are the pure in heart, for they shall see God."
—MATTHEW 5:8.

A PRAYER

Dear God, help us, as young folk, to keep clean, not only physically but mentally and spiritually.

Teach us to follow the example of Jesus that we may refrain from saying words that would hurt. Keep us from doing things that would soil our character.

Give us the strength to resist all temptations, and grant us the sense of right at all times, that our example may bring joy to those around us, as did the life of Jesus, our Lord. Amen.

A Message from Our Bible

"Blessed are the poor in spirit; for theirs is the kingdom of heaven.

Blessed are they that mourn; for they shall be comforted.

Blessed are the meek; for they shall inherit the earth.

Blessed are they which do hunger and thirst after righteousness; for they shall be filled.

Blessed are the merciful; for they shall obtain mercy.

Blessed are the pure in heart; for they shall see God.

Blessed are the peacemakers; for they shall be called the children of God.

Blessed are they which are persecuted for righteousness' sake; for theirs is the kingdom of heaven.

Blessed are ye, when men shall revile you, and persecute you, and shall say all manner of evil against you falsely, for my sake.

Rejoice, and be exceeding glad; for great is your reward in heaven; for so persecuted they the prophets which were before you."—MATTHEW 5:3–12.

FILMS

I WONDER how many of you young folks own a camera. I hope you all do, for taking pictures is a nice hobby to have, and it's not too expensive, either, if you are careful as to what you take! Just be sure it will make a nice picture and one you will want to show.

When I first got my camera I wanted to take a lot of pictures, so I did and when I had the film developed, I saw the beautiful scenes I had taken but in many cases the whole picture was not so beautiful because somehow I had overlooked the old shed which was in the background of one—and an old telephone pole in another and a scrawny old cat in the side foreground of another!

You see a film unexposed in the camera, is very sensitive and will catch all the objects in front of it, many of which you might not notice unless you are very careful.

It's like playing with a boy who has the measles, . . . you have a good time and enjoy the fun of his company, but usually you have to take the measles along with it.

In using your camera, after you get used to it, you take only pictures that have beautiful background and foreground. You don't want to spoil the object by finding you have exposed the film to something ungainly beside it.

Paul once said "Ye are the temple of God." He might also have said that we are like films in a camera, for whatever we expose ourselves to becomes a part of us. That is why as Christians we try to keep away from evil deeds and evil words so that the picture of our character will be beautiful and good, and we won't ever be ashamed to have people see us and hear us wherever we may be.

"Ye are the temple of God."—I CORINTHIANS 3:16.

A PRAYER

DEAR God, help us to realize our own responsibilities, and make us see that we must live for thee.

Teach us to think right thoughts that our lives may reflect Christian love as Jesus taught us.

As Jesus showed that he was clearly made in thy likeness, help us to so speak and act that we may reveal thee to many who are thoughtless and indifferent. Make us trustworthy through Jesus our Lord. Amen.

A MESSAGE FROM OUR BIBLE

"Every man's work shall be made manifest: for the day shall declare it, because it shall be revealed by fire; and the fire shall try every man's work of what sort it is.

Know ye not that ye are the temple of God, and that the Spirit of God dwelleth in you?

If any man defile the temple of God, him shall God destroy; for the temple of God is holy, which temple ye are."—I CORINTHIANS 3:13, 16–17.

FILTERS

WHEN your mother wants to wash away the sand from the strawberries she picked in the garden, she puts them in a strainer and pours water over them. The berries remain in the strainer and the sand is all washed out through the holes.

In percolating coffee, the coffee grounds are placed in a strainer-like receptacle, and when the water boils, it comes up over the coffee and goes out through the small holes.

In about every car there is a gadget called an oil filter. Pure, clean oil is poured into the car engine. This oil works its way in among the many ball bearings and a thin film of oil keeps the metal gears apart just enough so they will not wear out by rubbing against each other. Tiny particles of dirt get into this oil as it flows among the gears,—so, as it circulates around, it runs through a filter,—a strainer-like device which catches the dirt but allows the clean pure oil to flow on its way.

What happens when you hear someone tell a lie or say something bad about a friend of yours? Do you let it pass right along through you and start telling it to someone else? Or do you try to stop it and say a good word that ought to be said. I think our ears can act as filters for the things that people say.

Our eyes, too, can be filters when we see people doing things that are wrong. By our example we can try to influence them to lead cleaner, purer lives that their character, and ours, may be kept unharmed.

Jesus taught us the way of right living. Let us always follow his example and keep clean in all our words and deeds through the filtering control of God's love.

"The Lord will rescue me from every evil."—II TIMOTHY 4:18.

A PRAYER

Our Father, help us live clean lives. Teach us thy truth and help us discard any wrong ideas that may be suggested to us. Give us strength to stand firmly for the right, and to refuse to use words which are unkind and harmful.

Grant that we may so live, each day, that others may be happier,—that the love of Jesus may flow into our community so as to cleanse it from all evil.

Bless the children of other lands. Keep them secure, —safe from harm, hunger and destitution, and give us a generous spirit and the wisdom to help them be free from suffering. May thy peace and love be in us to give. Amen.

A Message from Our Bible

"Preach the word; be instant in season, out of season; reprove, rebuke, exhort, with all longsuffering and doctrine.

The Lord stood with me, and strengthened me; that by me the preaching might be fully known——

And the Lord shall deliver me from every evil work, and will preserve me unto his heavenly kingdom; to whom be glory for ever and ever."—II Timothy 4:2, 17–18.

FLEA FENCES

THERE are places, even in America, where there is a great deal of poverty. People are so poor they live in very shabby shacks with no windows, and ill-fitting doors. I have seen seven little dirty-faced boys and girls living with their parents and grandparents in a two or three room shack that one would scarcely keep hens in. In fact in this particular house, the hens, along with two dogs and several goats, spent a great many of the cooler nights, I was told.

That, of course, meant a lot of fleas! In talking with the missionary minister around in that vicinity, I learned that many of the people living under these conditions built fences to keep the fleas out of their humble homes. What, in the world, could a flea fence be?

Well, actually it was a goat fence! You see, the fleas were on the goats, so if the goats were fenced out the fleas stayed out with them!

There are a lot of things, like fleas, that can't be stopped by fences.

Hateful thoughts and ideas sometimes come into your mind and you express them by the use of words that come out of your mouth. Try and think of your lips as a fence against letting those words out for people to hear and then your thoughts won't hurt anyone.

Bad habits are pretty hard to get rid of but you can stop doing the thing that is forming a habit in you—and pretty soon there will be no habit at all.

Like fleas, evil words, bad habits, and wrong deeds can be stopped by stopping the carriers.

"According to the multitude of thy tender mercies blot out my transgressions."—PSALM 51:1.

A PRAYER

Our Father, we thank thee for thy goodness expressed in so many ways. In Jesus we see thee before us and hear thy words of wisdom. In Him thy teachings have been made plain.

Grant that cleanness of mind and pureness of heart may mean more to the youth of our community than selfish advancement. Help young folks to know the truth and give them strength to live it in their daily contacts.

Forgive us, Lord, when we fail and grant us the will to withstand temptations. Amen.

A Message from Our Bible

"Have mercy upon me, O God, according to thy lovingkindness: according to the multitude of thy tender mercies blot out my transgressions.

Wash me thoroughly from mine iniquity, and cleanse me from my sin.

Create within me a clean heart, O God; and renew a right spirit within me."—Psalm 51:1–2, 10.

GLASS

THE other day I stood on the sidewalk looking at a store window display of men's suits. They seemed to be orange in color which was very strange indeed. However, I realized right away that I was looking through a window covered with orange colored celophane.

I went inside and found that every display case had different colored glass through which I looked at the contents. Of course, as I looked through the blue glass everything looked dark, and as I looked through the rose glass all the things were rose in color, and so on as I glanced through many colors.

However, before buying any article I preferred seeing it under natural conditions and not through colored glass.

Sometimes at a theatre you see the beautiful costumes change color right before your eyes! First they are yellow, then blue and bright red and so on through many colors. Well there is nothing magic about it. You see, it is done by a revolving colored glass shutter in front of a spotlight which is trained on the figures.

That's the way some people see the world and the work they have to do. Bill sees people as through dark glasses and so everything seems dark and gloomy and discouraging to him.

Mae is selfish and sees life as through rose glass and never seems to take anything seriously, she is always joking and rather light in her thinking. Mari sees life as it is,—hardships and discouragements are all around her, but as she mingles with her friends she sees the real beauty of joy and happiness and reflects this attitude in her own life, and so radiates a loveliness of character that this world needs right now. Jesus saw life that way, and because of him, though he suffered much, others found peace and a richer life.

"Now we see through a glass darkly, but then face to face."—I CORINTHIANS 13:12.

A PRAYER

Our Father of mercies and comfort, we turn to thee in joy and in sadness, in health and in pain. We seek thy blessing, O God, and ask for strength.

In our service of Communion may we feel thy presence in the love of thy Son Jesus Christ.

As he lived, may we also be able to live that the truth of his gospel may prevail and establish peace on the earth.

Bless our missionaries as they lay the foundation of Christianity in many lands, entrusted with thy Spirit, sent by us. Help them in their task, direct them in their consecrated service.

Give counsel to our young folks and teach them, through home and Church, thy ever enduring truths as shown in the love of Jesus. Amen.

A Message from Our Bible

"Love suffereth long and is kind; love envieth not; love vaunteth not itself, is not puffed up,

Doth not behave itself unseemly, seeketh not her own, is not easily provoked, thinketh no evil;

Rejoiceth not in iniquity, but rejoiceth in the truth;

Beareth all things, believeth all things, hopeth all things, endureth all things.

Love never faileth;

Now we see through a glass darkly; but then face to face; now I know in part; but then shall I know even as also I am known."—I Corinthians 13:4–8, 12.

HIEROGLYPHICS

SOME years ago I visited the South-West portion of our United States and saw many rocks which had on them crudely carved pictures, and arrow signs or a pointing finger. They were very much worn characters but I expect that a few centuries ago the Indians who traveled in that country depended upon these messages for their direction and possibly for their warrior deeds.

In Egypt where explorers have recently unearthed whole cities, men have been able to tell us about that early civilization by reading the carved pictures and characters which are called Hieroglyphics.

Out in Hollywood I saw a place where many people have put their hands in soft cement and after it hardened, there was left the impression, permanently made, for the people to see and wonder about as they tour our country two hundred years from now! I wonder what people will look like in the year 2152 A.D. How will they be dressed?

Shorthand is a kind of modern hieroglyphic writing with its lines, curves, hooks and dots.

Every Sunday in church and probably every school day you might say you read hieroglyphics when you sing the hymns and songs, for the notes are written in the form of symbols. It would be pretty difficult to write out every note in regular longhand.

Hieroglyphics are characters or pictures which convey meaning, representing ideas or sounds.

So let us say that we are hieroglyphics for God! Let us be sure that we are Christians so that when others see us, and watch the way we act, they will be led to Christ.

"For this is the will of God in Christ Jesus. . . ."—I THESSALONIANS 5:18.

A PRAYER

Our Father, show us how to speak for thee. Help us be hands and feet for thee to carry thy gospel message to all young folks in the world.

Bless the children who are hungry and fearful. Protect them, dear Lord, and give them happiness and peace.

We thank thee for our homes, and for our churches. Help us make them happy places as we express thy love in our families and among our many friends. In Jesus name we ask. Amen.

A Message from Our Bible

"See that none render evil for evil unto any man; but ever follow that which is good, both among yourselves, and to all men.

Rejoice evermore.

Pray without ceasing.

In every thing give thanks: for this is the will of God in Christ Jesus concerning you.

Prove all things; hold fast that which is good.

Abstain from all appearances of evil.

And the very God of peace sanctify you wholly: and I pray God your whole spirit and soul and body be preserved blameless unto the coming of our Lord Jesus Christ."—I Thessalonians 5:15–18, 21–23.

HINGES

WHAT was the first thing you thought of when you saw this word, "Hinges"?

The first thing I think of when I hear or see the word, is "squeaks." I wonder if you have any door in your house that squeaks when you open it? Or a box cover?

The reason we hear doors squeak is because the hinges are seldom oiled until they *do* squeak! I hope you never disobey your parents, but some boys and girls do, sometimes, and do not run the errand they are told to. They are scolded for their neglect and severely punished.

Obedience, like the oil that keeps the hinges from squeaking,—keeps you happy, and also keeps your parents happy,—and then everything runs smoothly. You *have* to do the errand anyway; you might as well do it without squeaking!

Another thing of interst about Hinges is that one part is screwed to the wall, or box,—and then the door is attached to the other part so that it swings easily back and forth. When you visit your little friend how easily the front door swings out to let you in!

I hope none of you will ever be like the grouchy old hermit I once knew who boarded up all the windows and doors of his old shack, except one, and he kept a padlock on that!

Be friendly and happy. Just as the door of your house swings open easily because the hinges are well oiled—so, attach yourself to God; speak and act the way He would want you to, at all times. Keep the oil of the love and teachings of Jesus always ready in your heart, that other children who come to play with you will want to join you in the unselfish Christian way of living for Christ and his Church.

"Enter into his gate with thanksgiving and into his courts with praise."—PSALM 100:4.

A PRAYER

Our Father, God, we thank thee for the assurance of thy love, kind in its forgiveness, just in its reality. Teach us thy great truth and help us see more clearly, not only thy gifts to us, but ways by which we may daily serve thee and honor thy name.

Help us heed thy call to become more and more useful to more and more people. Bless, through us, young folks in every land. Give them food, dear Lord, using us as thy hands to feed them.

Give them confidence and security, using us as the expression of thy love. Help them to know thy great love by first seeing in us thy spirit of truth.

May thy rich blessing rest with our homes, that through them our community may know happiness and radiate it to the world. Amen.

A Message from Our Bible

"Make a joyful noise unto the Lord, all ye lands. Serve the Lord with gladness; Come before his presence with singing.

Enter into his gates with thanksgiving, And into his courts with praise; Give thanks unto him, and bless his name.

For the Lord is good; his lovingkindness endureth for ever, And his faithfulness unto all generations."—Psalm 100:1–2, 4–5.

HOUR GLASS TIME

NOT long ago, I stood watching the sand slowly sift through one of those three-minute egg timers and it reminded me of the Hour Glass which was actually used many years ago to tell the passing of the hours. It looked like an ordinary tall glass pulled together in the middle and closed at both ends. It took just one hour for the grains of sand to run through from the top half into the lower half. When the last bit of sand had gone through someone had to be on hand to turn the glass over, and the process was repeated.

Always, until now, days have been measured by hours!

However, almost everything else is measured by years. So if I look into the mouth of a horse I can tell approximately by its teeth, how many years old it is!

I used to help saw down great pine trees and wonder how long it took for certain ones to grow that big—some of them as much as three feet in diameter! So, while resting from sawing, I would count the rings as revealed on some large tree stump. Some rings were close together and others wide apart depending on the wet or dry season that year. The number of rings represented the number of years that tree had lived. If many hot, dry years came along, one right after another, it was hard to count the rings, they were so close together. The value of a tree or a horse is in the way it has lived.

People are like that—you may be seven or ten, twenty-two or eighty in years but I want to know how many golden grains of kindness, of helpfulness and sacrifice and love have gone through your life. What have you really done for Jesus? That's your real age. You live, not in years but in hourly deeds of Christian service.

"Blessed is he that doeth righteousness at all times."
—PSALM 106:3.

A PRAYER

Dear God, help us to so clearly understand thy love for us that we will give some time each day to thoughts of thee.

Teach us the way of Jesus as he lived among the people of his time that we may grow more like him. Teach us to pray as he prayed, for other people. Keep us from being selfish or jealous, and may all our days and years be happy because we know thee and trust thee, and because we, like him, seek to help people around us who are in need.

May our years be known by the service we render. Amen.

A Message from Our Bible

"Praise ye the Lord. Oh give thanks unto the Lord; for he is good; For his lovingkindness endureth for ever.

Who can utter the mighty acts of the Lord, Or show forth all his praise?

Blessed are they that keep justice, And he that doeth righteousness at all times."—Psalm 106:1–3.

A PAPER HOUSE

I saw a house last summer, built almost entirely of newspapers. Every piece of furniture was made of paper. And people lived in this Paper house.

It was built several years ago having been started by Mr. Elis F. Stenman with the help of his family, in 1922. A bare framework of wood was set up and then newspapers were dipped in some kind of secret formula and glued into place. The ceiling and walls are 215 newspapers thick and you can read the papers as well as the day they were printed.

There is the paper piano. A paper clock is made of newspapers from every State Capitol in the United States. The chairs are of paper, and a nice big desk is constructed wholly with newspapers telling the story, day by day, of Col. Charles A. Lindbergh's history making flight.

The secret of the process used by Mr. Stenman may never be revealed, but the fact remains that they took ordinary, easy-to-tear newspapers on which were words easily smudged and erased, and put them through some secret process which made them strong enough for house building material, and durable enough to last these many years, a house serviceable enough to live in and the news items still capable of being clearly read.

How true it is with us,—no matter how weak or unworthy, or incapable or untalented you and I may think we are, we can be made strong and more useful if we will but prepare ourselves by the single process of close association with God.

If we will but process,—train—ourselves in the love of Jesus, praying and learning of God, we will be made strong, and more worthy, and useful as we try to be his messengers.

"Thou therefore, my son, be strong in the grace that is in Christ Jesus."—II Timothy 2:1.

A PRAYER

DEAR Jesus, help us live the kind of life thou didst lead. We know we are not as worthy as thou,—or as capable, because we are so often weak and negligent.

Make us strong, dear Lord, and keep us faithful and dependable that people may trust us.

Guard us against wrong doing, or speaking angrily, and guide us in the right that in some way the world may be better because of us.

Grant us thy protecting care through Jesus our Lord. Amen.

A MESSAGE FROM OUR BIBLE

"You then, my son, be strong in the grace that is in Christ Jesus,

Take your share of suffering as a good soldier of Christ Jesus.

No soldier on service gets entangled in civilian pursuits, that he may please him who hath chosen him to be a soldier.

And if a man strive for masteries, he is not crowned, except he strive lawfully.

Consider what I say; and the Lord give thee understanding in all things."—II TIMOTHY 2:1, 3, 4, 5, 7.

HOUSES

LET us take a look at some of the houses we all have seen.

I looked over an expanse of water at Alcatraz once some time ago. How bare were the walls. It looked terribly cold with the iron bars and small rooms. I was glad to turn my eyes to happier objects.

I have seen some very beautiful homes, rich in color and lovely in architecture. Expensive rugs were on the floors and wonderful furniture in every room, beautiful gardens and a high stone wall around it all. So ornate were these houses I would feel almost afraid to move about in them. You feel that there must be a sign somewhere near the front door: "Please remove your shoes before you step in on our rugs." Yet they were houses where people lived.

And then I go into your house. It's nice and clean. There are chairs that invite me to sit down. Of course, there is a ball or a top on the floor that Junior forgot to pick up. Books and newspapers, etc. are lying around on the table or a chair. The pictures on the wall are the kind I like to see, and I can smell candy cooking in the kitchen and only hope it will be ready to eat before I leave! This is a house where people live but I also can say it's a home. The people there are friendly, happy, and greet me with a warm welcome.

In such a "home" one seldom even sees the "house." The general atmosphere of a house expresses the personalities and wholesomeness of those who live inside.

Jesus tells us that our bodies are just the houses in which we live. Our color, our stature, our weight do not matter. It's the character, the Christian spirit, of the person who lives inside that makes our house a home.

"Ye are the temple of God."—I CORINTHIANS 3:16.

A PRAYER

WE THANK thee, our Father, for the assurance of thy protective care. We thank thee for thy presence in our homes, and for the love thou didst bestow upon us in thy Son Jesus Christ.

Teach us to be thoughtful and considerate of one another in our homes and at school and help us be more Christian in our daily attitude. Keep us from anger and spite, and make us willing workers in thy church. We ask all this in Jesus' name. Amen.

A MESSAGE FROM OUR BIBLE

"Every man's work shall be made manifest: for the day shall declare it, because it shall be revealed by fire; and the fire shall try every man's work of what sort it is.

Know ye not that ye are the temple of God, and that the Spirit of God dwelleth in you?

If any man defile the temple of God, him shall God destroy; for the temple of God is holy, which temple ye are."—I CORINTHIANS 3:13, 16–17.

HYDRANTS

ONCE or twice I have seen men testing water hydrants, opening each one to see if the water flows from them all right. I noticed, what seemed rather strange to me at first, that the water did not spout high into the air but just came out without very much force.

You see, a hydrant isn't very useful to a house on fire unless a small hose is attached to it forcing the water through a small nozzle.

It works the same way with your lawn hose, the smaller the nozzle the higher the stream will rise. Place your finger over half the water outlet and it comes out with greater force.

Have you ever seen the Connecticut River? It is a wide and beautiful stream and in some places it is so wide you hardly see it flow. But there is one place in New Hampshire where it flows through a very narrow gorge between two hills and the powerful force of its flow is tremendous as it goes through this small outlet.

Now, when we talk about God we know that he is everywhere—"the world is his and all they who dwell therein." Even in such places where people have never heard of God, He is there waiting for them to accept Him. The reason so many people do not know Jesus is because no one has told them about him.

You see, water from the hydrant, to be of any use, must be conveyed by a small hose. So it is, my young friends, if God is to be known and understood by unchristian and non-Christian people, then you as one Christian boy or girl must carry the message of his love and of Christ's goodness and sacrifice to them. Only by your individual voice and acts can God's love put out the fires of hate and greed in the world, and bring peace.

"I can do all things through Christ who strengtheneth me."—PHILIPPIANS 4:13.

A PRAYER

Dear God, our Father, for the love that flows out from thee we give thanks. For the joy it gives the individual as it comes into the heart carrying happiness and peace to many around us, we thank thee.

Help us to see our opportunities for service, and, brushing aside our own unneeded wants, grant that we may always rush to the aid of those in trouble.

Keep us from arrogance and unfriendliness and teach us the true Christian purpose in living as Jesus exemplified, daily.

Forgive our selfish way and grant that we may freely give, that suffering may be no more. Keep us, thy children, from evil thoughts and wrong conduct, and let us be channels by which thy love and truth may enter all lives to guide their way. Amen.

A Message from Our Bible

"Whatsoever things are true, whatsoever things are honest, whatsoever things are just, whatsoever things are of good report; if there be any virtue and if there be any praise, think on these things.

I can do all things through Christ which strengtheneth me."—Philippians 4:8, 13.

ICE

I EXPECT everyone of you likes ice cream, and in the summer, during the hot days, you doubtless eat a lot of it. It takes a lot of ice to make ice cream and a lot more to keep it from melting.

Sometimes mother puts ice cubes in your glass of water or milk. How refreshing and cooling it is as you drink it.

When Dad brings home a basket of trout he just caught while on a fishing trip, he puts them on ice so they will be nice and fresh when mother gets ready to cook them, for ice keeps food from spoiling. That is what refrigerators are for!

An ice bag is sometimes placed around your neck when you have a sore throat.

But some morning you may rush out of the house pell-mell for school—late as usual—and as you step on the sidewalk—wham-o!, and you have a sore spot, or perhaps a broken bone!

Ice is good or bad according to our use of it. In the summer we want it; in the winter we don't!

So much of life is just like that. The words you speak —they can be for good or for evil depending on how we use them. The money we have—we can be generous and help people in need, or we can be selfish and hoard it and cheat others so as to get more.

Fire is a wonderful thing to have in your stove to cook with and to keep you warm, but if a fire is started out in a great forest, what destruction it leaves!

God has given us so many useful things, let us always use them for good.

"Let anyone who thinks that he stands take heed lest he fall."—I CORINTHIANS 10:12.

A PRAYER

We seek thy blessing, O Lord, because of our needs, knowing thy great love and forgiving spirit.

Help us to be patient, for we would have others patient with us. Help us to show the spirit of love in a world where we need the strength of thy great love. Make us worthy of the name of 'Christian' and lead us to be more aggressive with thy gospel truths, in order to point the way to a more Christ-like community.

Be our example, dear Lord, and help us to be as thou art in exemplifying the true values of life. Give the young folk an understanding of the meaning of thy love through the knowledge of the life of Jesus, and help us all to become more like Him in action and speech. Amen.

A Message from Our Bible

"Wherefore let him that thinketh he standeth take heed lest he fall.

There hath no temptation taken you but such as is common to man; But God is faithful, who will not suffer you to be tempted above that ye are able; but will with the temptation also make a way to escape, that ye may be able to bear it."—I Corinthians 10:12–13.

IN TUNE

ALMOST every school has an orchestra and some churches do, and I expect many of you play some instrument. I hope you all learn to play the piano. The most popular boy in any college is the one who can play the piano.

When I'm planning to listen to an evening program of orchestral music I want to arrive early so that I can hear the members "tune up." It's usually the pianist, who leads off by striking a note or chord and then all the other instruments begin to sound. After a while each player is satisfied that his instrument is in tune with the piano which of course means in tune with each other.

There used to be a time, many, many years ago,—in your great grandparents day, when churches had no organ or piano to set the tune for the hymns. The people of the congregation just started right in singing, and I expect there were plenty of discordant sounds! Then later someone got up front with a pitch-pipe by which the right note was sounded and everybody would sing in tune with him and with each other.

I've heard children who would seem to be out of tune, not only in singing, or playing in an orchestra at some school event, but in their relation to each other when they were supposed to be playing baseball, or hockey, or hide and seek or just standing around talking. Arguments begin, disagreements start and tempers get pretty short. Each child wants his own way so he yells for it in very discordant tones and unmusical words and the sound is not pretty.

Pray a lot, speak kindly, and be thoughtful of others, and you will find it easier to keep in tune with your young playmates.

"Even as Christ forgave you, so also do ye."—COLOSSIANS 3:13.

A PRAYER

Our Heavenly Father, in thy great goodness and power, keep us in tune with thy will and purpose.

Help us not to be so interested in the world pleasures as to neglect the vital issue of living our life for thee.

Direct the purpose of our individual lives to making this world and this community a finer, more Christian place in which to dwell. Give our young folk a real sense of true direction and purpose for their lives and lead them in their daily prayers that in finding themselves in tune with thee they may grow to live in harmony with each other.

We pray that our lives may count for the establishment of peace among the peoples of this world. To this purpose live thou in our hearts, O God, as in Jesus Christ our Lord. Amen.

A Message from Our Bible

"Put on therefore, as the elect of God, holy and beloved, bowels of mercies, kindness, humbleness of mind, meekness, longsuffering;

Forbearing one another, and forgiving one another, if any man have a quarrel against any; even as Christ forgave you, so also do ye.

Above all these things put on charity, which is the bond of perfectness.

Let the peace of Christ rule in your hearts. . . ."—Colossians 3:12–15.

30

LABELS

I WAITED in a long line at the post office the other day to mail a package to my Marine son, Bob, who is in Korea and as I drew nearer the window I could hear the postman ask "Anything breakable or perishable?"

Upon being told what was in the package he would stamp it with the label "Book" or "Mdse." or "Glass." Labels, on a package, tell the nature of what is inside.

Usually you write your name on the package or letter in the upper left hand corner. That means you are inside—at least your thoughts, your love, perhaps your sacrifice—anyway it's yours until it is received by your friend.

I go into your home sometimes—especially if you are sick, and there is one thing I always look for! I'm not interested in the chairs or tables, or the kind of bed you are in or even the radio you have, but I do look for a religious picture on the wall or on your table. I hope every one of you boys and girls has a picture of Jesus somewhere in your room. It's a label that tells people something about you, just as a newspaper clipping of Ted Williams or Don Newcombe tells of your interest in sports.

There are many other labels attached to you that tell me the kind of a person you are.

The way you treat a stray dog or cat tells me a lot about your character. Your love for birds,—the kind of books you like to read.

Most of all your loyalty to your church and your church group labels you as dependable. When you show you are faithful to God and his work through the church, then people know you to be a real Christian.

"Jesus Christ is the same yesterday, today and forever."—HEBREWS 13:8.

A PRAYER

Dear God, help us see, clearly, our duty toward thee, our parents and to all who lead us as we learn about the ways of life.

We thank thee for home and church where we are taught how to live like Jesus.

We are really thankful for the school and our teachers, under whose guidance we grow in knowledge and understanding.

We thank thee too for happy hours and restful nights and for the joy of a new day; may they all be filled with peace and contentment by the strength of the love of Jesus in our hearts.   Amen.

A Message from Our Bible

"Remember them which have the rule over you, who have spoken unto you the word of God; whose faith follow, considering the end of their conversation.

Jesus Christ the same yesterday, and today, and for ever.

By him therefore let us offer the sacrifice of praise to God continually, that is, the fruit of our lips, giving thanks to his name.

But to do good and to communicate forget not; for with such sacrifices God is well pleased."—Hebrews 13:7–8, 15–16.

31

LAMPS

I WONDER how many of you children ever saw an oil lamp. A room lighted with a kerosene lamp would seem pretty dark as compared to an electric light bulb hanging from the ceiling. The oil of course was in the bowl and a tape-like cloth called a wick was so placed as to allow one end to rest in the kerosene while the other came up through the lamp and was lighted. You see this wick drew the oil up and kept the light blazing steadily. I recall we had a lamp once with two wicks and sometimes one would go out and the room would be darker. You see this wick was shorter than the other and when the lamp bowl was only half full of oil it wouldn't quite reach so it got black and smelly and finally the flame went out while the other continued to shed its light.

Sometimes electric bulbs go out too, for the same general reason—the filament wears out and no longer has contact with the electric power and the room becomes darker.

The oil was in the lamp bowl. The electric power was available but the wick was short, the filament was broken from the current, so, no light!

Sometimes we are too short to reach God. Short tempered when someone disagrees with us and we just sputter out some unkind words.

Boys get into fights over very small matters, like getting mad at the umpire in a ball game. Try keeping yourself always in touch with God, for in Him is the source of your strength of character.

Just as the oil is necessary to the wick in order to shed a true light, so God is necessary to you if you are to be trustworthy boys and girls shining for Jesus in true Christian character.

"Then all those virgins arose, and trimmed their lamps."—MATTHEW 25:7.

A PRAYER

DEAR God, our Father, we acknowledge thy presence around about us, and within, at all times. Help us to sense it upon every occasion and in every venture. May we truly be led by thy will.

Help us, O God, to overcome and withstand mental and physical pressures and maintain a clean heart and a right spirit.

Forgive our shortcomings and give us the added strength of thy love. Bless the young folks of our community and as we build programs for world relationships among the nations may we think of them more than ourselves. Give them clear vision and right thinking.

Help those who are ill in body, mind or spirit and lead them to find contentment in thee, and grant, O God, that thy spirit of love may prevail as lived in Jesus our Lord. Amen.

A MESSAGE FROM OUR BIBLE

"Then shall the kingdom of heaven be likened unto ten virgins, which took their lamps, and went forth to meet the bridegroom.

And five of them were wise, and five were foolish.

They that were foolish took their lamps, and took no oil with them;

But the wise took oil in their vessels with their lamps."
—MATTHEW 25:1–4.

32

LIGHTS

THERE is a hymn which I like very much—it's an old one and we used to sing it a lot in church years ago—"Let the Lower Lights be Burning." The setting of the words of that hymn is in Norway where the west coast is indented and hazardous.

In order that the fisherman at night out at sea, may find his way to his port a light is set high up on a hill in back of his house to mark a straight course for him. However, as he nears the land he is unable to see the high light any more so his wife or some member of his family places a light in a window of their home to guide the home coming boat to the proper slip.

All along the shore these Lower Lights are burning at night to guide the ships and the men to safety and to the warmth of home.

Our Bible tells us that a bright high light led the Shepherds to Bethlehem where they were told of the birth of Jesus. Later a great star high in the sky guided the Wise men to the city. Upon their arrival the star was no longer adequate. They had to inquire where the Child Jesus was and they were directed to the place of his abode.

You see, these people who directed the Shepherds and later the Wise men, to Jesus, were in reality the Lower Lights. Later, when the Shepherds left the stable home, and as they went back to tend their sheep, they praised God and told others of this Christ Child. They were the Lower Lights to many, showing them the way to God,— Home.

Jesus, the great high light of the world, asks us to be Lower Lights as his guides.

"I am the Light of the world; he that followeth me shall not walk in darkness, but shall have the light of life."—JOHN 8:12.

A PRAYER

O Thou who art the Light of the world, help us to receive it into our hearts. Thou who art the Way, help us to follow in the footsteps of the Master.

So many times we feel ourselves "at sea," not understanding how to solve our problems. Help us to see more clearly that our parents are right when they deny us the things we seem to want.

May thy spirit of love teach us to see more clearly in thy light, and give us the right sense of direction that we may follow the way of truth through the leadership of Jesus Christ our Lord. Amen.

A Message from Our Bible

"In the beginning was the Word, and the Word was with God, and the Word was God.

The same was in the beginning with God.

All things were made by him, and without him was not any thing made that was made.

In him was life; and the life was the light of men.

And the light shineth in darkness; and the darkness comprehended it not.

There was a man sent from God, whose name was John.

The same came for a witness, to bear witness of the Light, that all men through him might believe."—JOHN 1:1–7.

33

A MAGIC BOX

MANY years ago, a man, while traveling in India made a practice of collecting trinkets peculiar to that country. One evening as he was walking in the dusk of twilight, he saw a bright light on the ground; going over to it he picked up the object, which shed this light, and it proved to be a box.

He took the box to his room and it shone brilliantly all night.—The next day he learned that it was a "Magic Box."

The next night he looked at his box and noticed that no light came from it! So he picked it up and discovered the cover would open and inside he found this note: "If you will put me in the light all day, I'll shine for you all night."

Sure enough—it absorbed the sun's light in the day-time and radiated it at night.

This incident made me think of the times, when I was a boy on the farm, when I used to take a hot soapstone and put it in my bed at night to keep me warm when the thermometer outside went down to forty below zero!

Even a candle or a lamp has to be lighted before it can give out its shining brightness at night.

That bicycle pump has to be filled with air before it can push it into your tire.

So it is with us, before we can give the love of God, we must first receive it from Him. We must place our minds and our hearts before God in prayer and worship, and be filled with the love and teachings of Jesus and then we will want to shine for Him to help other people see the right more clearly.

"For God . . . hath shined in our hearts."—II Co-RINTHIANS 4:6.

[75]

A PRAYER

Dear Lord, please fill us with thy love, so that we may express it to all around us, and grant that thy spirit of happiness may so be implanted in our hearts that people will know us to be Christians, as we walk along the street.

Teach us to pray, dear God, that we may feel thy presence ever near us, so that we may impart thy spirit to all who seek to know thee.   Amen.

A Message from Our Bible

"For we preach not ourselves, but Christ Jesus the Lord; and ourselves your servants for Jesus' sake.

For God, who commanded the light to shine out of darkness, hath shined in our hearts, to give the light of the knowledge of the glory of God in the face of Jesus Christ."—II Corinthians 4:5–6.

34
A MAGNIFYING GLASS

When someone speaks of a magnifying glass I expect about the first thing you think of is a detective looking for clues! Or perhaps a jeweler with one of those gadgets he fits into one eye when he looks at the works in your watch. The glasses some people have to wear when they read are also magnifying glasses.

Maybe you are out looking for beautiful butterflies, or studying plant life.

What is it that the magnifying glass does for you anyway?

I expect your first answer would be that "it makes objects larger so you can see them better." That is not quite so, because a magnifying glass does not change the size of the object. It just increases your ability to see it better!

A telescope doesn't make the moon any larger but you can see it a lot plainer when you look through that tele-scope "magnifying glass." A magnifying glass seems to bring objects that are far away, right up close to you.

My hobby is collecting "Indian Head" pennies and I find that the date doesn't always show up large enough for me to tell what it is, so I use my magnifying glass and under it the date seems to be raised right up for me to read.

Now, God is always near us but we so often do not sense his presence because we don't look for him hard enough.

I like to think of prayer as a magnifying glass—it makes God seem nearer to me when I look for him in prayer.

When things go wrong, pray, and you will feel God close by you, ready to give you strength.

"O magnify the Lord with me . . . exalt his name."
—Psalm 34:3.

A PRAYER

GREAT God, our Heavenly Father, thou art ever near us, ready to help in times of stress with our problems.

Help us to see thee, even as thou art. In thy great love may we see thee through eyes of love and so magnify thy name on the earth.

Give us wisdom that we may know the depth of thy understanding heart. Let our faith be so strong that we shall see thee in all thy true greatness.

Help the young people to think clearly, and by praying sincerely, to feel that thy love and care is very near to them. In the beauty and orderliness of nature thou dost show us more and more, the grandeur of thy plan for us. Teach us to beautify the world with peace and joy. Through Jesus Christ our Lord. Amen.

A MESSAGE FROM OUR BIBLE

"I will bless the Lord at all times; his praise shall continually be in my mouth.

My soul shall make her boast in the Lord; the meek shall hear thereof, and be glad.

Oh magnify the Lord with me, and let us exalt his name together.

I sought the Lord and he answered me, and delivered me from all my fears."—PSALM 34:1–4.

35

A MATCH

In one of my other books I told you about building fires without matches. Boy Scouts learn how to do this and it's a good thing to know, for you might get lost in the woods sometime and need a fire for a signal or for warmth.

When matches first were invented they were dangerous because the least friction against anything would set them ablaze.

Then came the box of safety matches which could be lighted on the box—but they could also be lighted if rubbed against glass!

Now we have safety matches on those cardboards.

The one thing about all matches is that they just don't burst into flame all by themselves. A match, to produce a light has to come into contact with something else—then it becomes useful, good for something.

It just occurs to me that you boys and girls are like the match. God wants you to be good and clean. He gives you talents and ability, but, merely possessing these qualifications is not enough. He wants you to use them and that means contact with others, helping people when you see they need a lift. Perhaps some boy or girl is shy—go and talk with him or her.

Perhaps he is of another color or nationality—be friendly. Perhaps she is new in your school,—speak to her and introduce her to others, and to your play. Possibly he is having trouble with his History lessons.—Spend a little time, go over it with him.

Live close to Jesus and let your life shine into other people's hearts to encourage them. A match gives no light of itself until it is stirred into action with a desire to be useful to someone.

"In him was life and the life was the light of men."—John 1:4.

A PRAYER

DEAR God, we thank thee for all the joy there is in the world. Help us spread happiness about us by being thoughtful and kind to the people we meet, by helping the elderly and the sick; by cheering those who are sad, through generous gifts to the poor.

Make us worthy of thy love and help us follow the example of thy son Jesus. As he was the Light of life, help us to be a light that will guide other young folks to thee, through the love of Jesus our Lord. Amen.

A MESSAGE FROM OUR BIBLE

"There was a man sent from God, whose name was John.

The same came for a witness, to bear witness of the Light, that all men through him might believe.

He was not that Light, but was sent to bear witness of that Light.

That was the true Light, which lighteth every man that cometh into the world.

As many as received him, to them gave he power to become the sons of God, even to them that believe on his name;"—JOHN 1:6–9, 12.

36

HOMOGENIZED MILK

WHEN I was a boy on the farm we kept a number of cows and I had all the milk I wanted to drink. I also liked a lot of butter so about once every week we made butter. Now, in order to make butter we had to have cream, so each night we would "set" the milk and place it in a cool place and the cream would rise to the top. Then we would draw off the skimmed milk—which now looked like blue water—and throw it away or give it to the pigs.

When your mother wants cream she goes out and buys some—or perhaps takes just a little from the top of the milk bottle and then shakes up the rest, mixing what is left of the cream with the milk.

I remember the first time I bought a bottle of milk with no cream showing on the top part. I looked at the label and read the word "Homogenized." It was processed in such a way that the cream remained a part of the milk as nature intended it to be without rising to the top. It had been put through a certain heating routine to reach this homogenized situation.

I'm not sure what kind of milk is best to buy for our use but I'm quite sure that people should be homogenized. They should be the same all the way through, at all times —dependable. Milk is most valuable as milk when it has the cream mixed right in with the rest of the fluid— in fact that really makes it milk!

I don't like to see boys and girls all cream and sweet one day, and the next day, because they don't have their own way, be solemn, blue and sour.

Furthermore, if you are like sweet cream when out in company don't be sour and uninteresting at home. Homogenize yourself—God sees you at home as well as at a party.

"Maintain the unity of the Spirit in the bond of peace." —EPHESIANS 4:3.

A PRAYER

Our God in Heaven, teach us to pray. Fill us with thy love that we may show forth thy spirit as we work and play together.

Give us a will to be consistent in all we do, applying thy truth at home as well as away.

Lead us in strength to be more like Jesus. Harmonize us to the way of His life and keep us consecrated to thee while we work and talk with each other.

Bless all who, in trouble, seek thy help; and grant to us the ability to relieve suffering, and to vanquish evil.

Bless our homes, dear Lord, where children learn the practice of thy love through courtesy and patience.

Strengthen us that we may do thy will, and speak thy truth, always. Amen.

A Message from Our Bible

"I . . . beseech you that ye walk worthy of the vocation wherewith ye are called,

With all lowliness and meekness, with longsuffering, forbearing one another in love;

Endeavouring to keep the unity of the Spirit in the bond of peace.

There is one body and one Spirit, even as ye are called in one hope of your calling;

One Lord, one faith, one baptism,

One God and Father of all, who is above all, and through all, and in you all."—Ephesians 4 :1–6.

37

MIRRORS

MY YOUNG friends—what is a mirror?   I looked it up in the dictionary and discovered these words describing a mirror—"A glass that forms images by reflections" of objects.   So you stand before a mirror and you see an image—a picture or likeness of yourself or of someone or something near you.

This image you see may be a likeness of you but it never shows you exactly as other people see you, for a mirror is not quite 100% perfect.

You know I've read about people looking into a mirror and then breaking it, because they were disgusted with the image they saw there.   But breaking the mirror didn't change their appearance one single bit.

Not long ago my attention was drawn to two young men as we were riding some distance in a train.   One was continually adjusting his tie, and straightening his hat and sometimes combing his hair.   Evidently he was trying to make an impression—an image on other people's minds.

The other lad was reading a book which I found out to be the Bible.   He probably was a student in some school of Theology and was improving his time while on the train.

You see, by watching what those two boys were doing I got a very good image and understanding of the kind of lads they were.   I could see their character which really is what a person is, for the things you do and the words you use and like to hear or read show others the kind of person you are.

Glass mirrors will tell you of the smudge on your face but the Bible mirror will reveal your character, your thoughtfulness, your life as it should be.

"Beholding his natural face . . . he goes away and forgets."—JAMES 1:23, 24.

A PRAYER

DEAR Jesus, we thank thee for a happy day, and for the opportunities we have had to make others happy by our words and actions.

Bless our homes, dear God, and give joy to our parents, and help us contribute to their happiness.

We thank thee for the peace and quiet of night, with its playtime at home, and for rest through the hours until morning light, when sunshine again fills our hearts with refreshing faith.   Amen.

A MESSAGE FROM OUR BIBLE

"For if any be a hearer of the word, and not a doer, he is like unto a man beholding his natural face in a glass;

For he beholdeth himself, and goeth his way, and straightway forgetteth what manner of man he was.

But whoso looketh into the perfect law of liberty, and continueth therein, he being not a forgetful hearer, but a doer of the work, this man shall be blessed in his deed.

Pure religion and undefiled before God and the Father is this, To visit the fatherless and widows in their affliction, and to keep himself unspotted from the world."— JAMES I :23–25, 27.

38

NO SHADOW

I'M VERY sorry I cannot give credit to the person who wrote the following poetic lines,—the author's name was not given, but I do want to use it as the basis of my Parable to you today.

"Don't hunt after trouble, but look for success:
You'll find what you look for; don't look for distress,
If you see but your shadow, remember, I pray,
That the sun is still shining; but you're in the way."

An elderly man was hunting for something along the street gutter. Three boys came along and one asked: "Lost something, Mister?"

"Yes," said the man. "And I'll give you each a nickel if you find my ring."

The boys scrambled about for a while—then I heard one boy look up and say: "Mister, would you stand back a bit so the sun can shine in here—it might make it glisten so we can see it!"

The ring was finally found and each boy got his nickel.

Many times I've asked boys and girls why they don't like to study,—of course some do,—but many don't like to get at it, so they put it off as long as they can. The answer often is: "It's such drudgery." "There are so many other things we want to do!"

"Drudgery" is the shadow, caused by these "other things" which you want to do. All you have to do is to remove these other things from your thoughts for a while and the shadows will go away.

Keep all your shadows behind you. If you have a grudge, forget it. If someone says something he didn't mean, forgive him. Jesus did.

———

"For God is a sun and a shield—no good thing will he withhold from them that walk uprightly."—PSALM 84:11.

A PRAYER

DEAR God, we thank thee for Jesus, who lived so happily and so unselfishly. Grant that his teachings may guide us to right thinking and lead us to right doing.

Help us look toward thee and so see the beauty of life, and grant that no shadows of discord and unfriendliness come to make for unhappiness and misunderstanding. Amen.

A MESSAGE FROM OUR BIBLE

"For the Lord God is a sun and a shield; The Lord will give grace and glory;

No good thing will he withhold from them that walk uprightly.

O Lord of hosts, Blessed is the man that trusteth in thee."—PSALM 84:11–12.

39

OIL

ONE morning, several years ago, I recall that Mrs. Sargent plugged in the cord of the washing machine—but nothing happened! The motor just hummed very lightly but that was all. There was not power enough to turn the gears.

So I went to work on it, testing my mechanical ability! Very soon every light in the house was out of commission. So I called for help!

It took the expert about five minutes to tell me that the motor and gears needed oil. The fuses just would not turn those moving parts without oil to make them move smoothly.

I guess every boy who has a bicycle knows how important oil is. Without it the wheels tread with difficulty and the chain often snaps. I remember, when on the farm, as a boy, I used a wheelbarrow a lot, to carry things from one place to another. Sometimes the wheel would squeak and squawk so loudly that someone would call out "Why don't you oil that thing?"

As these squeaks in unoiled machinery are most disturbing, so frowns and grumbles on the part of one person seems to effect the whole household.

You come in out of sorts and pretty soon everyone near you is on edge and unhappy. And then you smile and say you are sorry and what a difference comes over everyone.

After oiling that washing machine all the fuses worked and the lights came on all over the house.

Keep yourselves well oiled with Christian love and kindness and consideration in your home and there will never be any blow-outs to disturb the happiness and peace that gives light and power to all who live there.

"Be tenderly affectioned one to another."—ROMANS 12:10.

A PRAYER

Dear Father, Merciful and loving God, we ask thee to hear our prayer of recognition and petition.

We thank thee for thy love and kindness expressed in so many ways around us; and grant that we may help one another as each day gives opportunities.

Make us strong in faith that we may be trustworthy as we go about our daily tasks.

Bless the young folks, dear Lord, as they meet the problems in their daily associations, and as they play together, may they learn the basic truth of working together. Bless our missionaries in every land and may their work be fruitful. Amen.

A Message from Our Bible

"Let love be without dissimulation. Abhor that which is evil; cleave to that which is good.

Be kindly affectioned one to another with brotherly love; in honor preferring one another;

Not slothful in business; fervent in spirit; serving the Lord;

Rejoicing in hope; patient in tribulation; continuing instant in prayer."—Romans 12 : 9–12.

40

ONE SNOWFLAKE

Dɪᴅ you ever pick up one single snowflake and hold it in the palm of your hand? How quickly it disappears and leaves just a tiny drop of water. If you picked that snowflake off the ground it may have left a bit of a smudge because when that pure clean white flake hit the earth it may have gotten into bad company and been soiled a little. We too have to watch out for that—we don't want bad company to hurt our character.

Let us think of that snowflake in the palm of your hand. It really is very powerful. Our history books tell us it stopped Napoleon's Army—and bogged down Hitler's vast horde. Of course many, many other snowflakes were added to the first one—and they kept piling up one by one 'til a great heavy blanket was laid over the land.

The power of one snowflake is tremendous—when you see the first snowflake in the fall it sends you hunting for your overshoes—perhaps, also, your skis when you think of the countryside as it will look in the morning!

One tiny snowflake—and the street department gets the snow-plows in readiness. With that first snowflake armies have been doomed.

Do you recall in the study of American history how one boy grew up and made all the difference in the world with our country. His name was George Washington. Another most important boy was Abraham Lincoln. Just one person leading the way and others following.

One Boy Jesus grew strong and kept faith with the will and love of God, and his influence on the world has been tremendous—and will continue to be as long as his following,—his Christian people,—will keep growing in numbers, and persist in wiping out all evil.

"And Jesus increased in wisdom and stature, and in favor with God and man."—Lᴜᴋᴇ 2:52.

A PRAYER

As we look out upon thy great universe, O God, and recognize how small we are, guide us in our thinking and show us the importance of one individual.

In thy son Jesus thou did'st use one person to redeem the whole world. Give us strength that we may do much toward making a better world by leading others to a better understanding of thy love.

Hear our prayer and make us worthy of being thy children. Amen.

A Message from Our Bible

"And it came to pass, that after three days they found him in the temple, sitting in the midst of the doctors, both hearing them, and asking him questions.

And when they saw him, they were amazed; and his mother said unto him, Son, why hast thou thus dealt with us? Behold, thy father and I have sought thee sorrowing.

And he said unto them, How is it that ye sought me? wist ye not that I must be about my Father's business? And Jesus increased in wisdom and stature, and in favor with God and man."—Luke 2:46, 48, 49, 52.

41

PEDESTALS

A PEDESTAL is a raised foundation upon which is placed a statue—so that people can look up to it as they pass by. The Statue of Liberty is resting on a pedestal. There she stands holding the torch high in her right hand and in her left, a book. That pedestal lifts her to the highest point in that area so that if she wanted to climb higher she couldn't.

You see, when a person is on a pedestal the only step he can take is *down!*

I've seen a lot of boys and girls who like to stand on pedestals—not the marble or granite or cement ones—but the pedestal of praise and honor. I'm thinking of a girl I know who is good in dramatics and after a reading she gave, many words of praise came to her. She stood on that pedestal for several weeks and she didn't feel the need of practice, and sure enough when she appeared before the public again she stepped down!

Mariam Bouroughs is one of the best violinists I have ever heard because she has never allowed herself to stand on a pedestal. On the contrary she has become highly respected and honored because she was generous, helpful and wholly unselfish and humble with her talent.

Maybe you can sing or play the piano or harmonica but always remember that other boys and girls can, too—or perhaps they are proficient in something else.

Don't let a little praise cause you, like a bantam rooster, to jump up and down with superior glee and land on a pedestal—you might have to step down.

Jesus said the greatest people are those who are humble—who keep practicing the love of Christ every day.

"Whoever humbles himself like this child he is the greatest in the Kingdom of heaven!"—MATTHEW 18:4.

A PRAYER

DEAR God, our Father, help us to keep humble in our relation to other people. If they praise us, keep us ever mindful that they are just as worthy of praise.

Grant, O Lord, that we may always try to do all things well. Help us understand ourselves that we may know how to keep strong, that we may do thy will.

Give to us the willingness to live for thee and for our friends. Give to us the desire to help displaced persons who have no place to live. Especially we pray for the children who lack and need the comforts and security of home.

Teach us thy truth, O God, and may we always live by it, and let the goodness of thy love direct us in all our ways. Amen.

A MESSAGE FROM OUR BIBLE

". . . Who is the greatest in the kingdom of heaven? And Jesus called a little child unto him, and set him in the midst of them.

And said, Verily I say unto you, Except ye be converted, and become as little children, ye shall not enter into the kingdom of heaven.

Whosoever therefore shall humble himself as this little child, the same is greatest in the kingdom of heaven."—MATTHEW 18:1–4.

42

PENNIES

ONE of my hobbies is the collection of Indian Head pennies.

As to the value of these pennies in the transaction of business, such as buying chewing gum or marbles, they are worth no more than the ordinary Lincoln penny. However, as with postage stamps, there is a dealers' market for them, and some are much more valuable than others, such as old or scarce ones.

The Indian Head penny, to be of added value must be unmutilated. I don't like to see any money with scars on it—as though someone tried to do harm to the U.S. Government. After all, money does represent our government and unless the words "The United States of America" and "One Cent" are stamped on these cent pieces their true value is nothing. They may be even counterfeit. The words "In God we trust" are of great importance, too, as found on many of our coins.

Every coin is worth the face value—and sometimes much more—if it is true to itself as defined, and it seems to become more valuable when it is scarce.

How true that is of people,—of boys and girls,—when there is a piece of hard work to do, everyone admires and appreciates the boy or girl who sticks to the job until it's done. So many have excuses, or quickly get tired and quit, but there is always someone who stands by who can be depended upon in the scarcity of helpers.

Out of all of Jesus' followers, twelve stood by and carried the message of the Gospel. Clean cut, unmutilated by unworthy deeds, stamped by the love of God, bright in service, therefore most valuable in the Christian plan of peace on earth.

"And those who were ready went in. . . ."—MAT-
THEW 25:10.

A PRAYER

In thee, O Lord, we place our trust and with thy help we solve the problems that come to us.

Guide us in our thinking when we find ourselves all mixed up. Help us reach our goal, but if we fail in this, give us courage to keep on trying.

Grant that young people everywhere may learn how to follow thee, dear Lord, and give their parents and those who rule, a sense of true justice and love that nations will know no more wars.

Bless thy church, O God, and the schools and all agencies of Christian relationship among all sects and races to the end that of love and justice and peace there may be no end. Amen.

A Message from Our Bible

". . . Behold the bridegroom cometh; go ye out to meet him.

Then all those virgins arose, and trimmed their lamps.

And the foolish said unto the wise, Give us of your oil; for our lamps are gone out.

But the wise answered, saying, Not so; lest there be not enough for us and you; but go ye rather to them that sell, and buy for yourselves.

Watch therefore; for ye know neither the day nor the hour wherein the Son of man cometh."—Matthew 25: 6–9, 13.

43
PENS

WHEN you boys and girls do your home work in arithmetic I expect you use pencils, but when a composition is called for by the teacher she probably instructs you to use a pen.

Many years ago when a person wanted to write something in ink he had to go out and catch a goose! At least, I'm told, that our great grandfathers, when they signed the great State papers, like the Declaration of Independence and our Constitution, did so with a quill pen dipped in ink. The quill was sharpened to a point and the point split part way up.

So you see if you lose your pen or spoil it, you can go out and catch a goose or a turkey and make your own. However, it's much simpler to ask Dad for five cents or a dollar or ten dollars and go to the corner drug store and buy one!

When the President of the United States signs an important paper he has a special pen—it may be gold tipped or diamond tipped, and then he just gives it to a friend who keeps it, I expect, as a prized souvenir.

However, whether it's a quill pen or a diamond tipped pearl handle fountain pen, if it is to leave words for future reading it has to be dipped in ink.

How often do you find yourself using a pen and suddenly realize no words are being made? So you dip it into the inkwell;—or shake it, if it's a fountain pen—and then give up and fill it.

That's just the way with you children—and older folks too—if you want people to think you are clean you must wash your face! If you want to help spread the love of God and have your friends really understand it through your actions you must, yourself, be filled with that Christlike Spirit of love and goodness.

"May the God of hope fill you with all joy and peace in believing. . . ."—ROMANS 15:13.

A PRAYER

Dear Lord, help us to realize our need of thee. Too often we think we are self-sufficient,—that we are always right. Help us to consider others, and keep us unselfish, and use us each day that whatever we do or say may help in some way to increase thy love in the hearts of the people we know.

Fill us with thy thoughts, O God, that we may give happiness and cheer to all who see us, and to all who live and play with us at home or in school. We pray in the love of Jesus. Amen.

A Message from Our Bible

"May the God of hope fill you with all joy and peace in believing, so that by the power of the Holy Spirit you may abound in hope.

I myself am satisfied about you, that you yourselves are full of goodness, filled with all knowledge, and able to instruct one another.

But on some points I have written to you very boldly by way of reminder, because of the grace given me by God to be a minister of Christ Jesus.

In Christ Jesus, then, I have reason to be proud of my work for God.

The God of peace be with you all."—Romans 15:13–17, 33.

44

PERFUMES

FOR over half an hour one dark night around midnight on a rather lonely road, I was held up—by a skunk! The nature of the road didn't allow me to go around him and the nature of the skunk warned me not to pass too near him so I waited until he left the road. Had I disturbed the lovely animal I'm sure I would have spent the rest of the night on the porch.

I suppose every girl has two or three bottles of perfume on her dresser. Possibly there might be found one hidden away in a boy's bureau drawer too! Anyway, I picked up a tiny bottle off Mrs. Sargent's dresser and opened the cap and a very lovely smelling aroma drew my undivided attention. She informed me that she had had that little vial for a long time. The liquid doesn't seem to evaporate very fast even though the perfume fills the room when the cap is removed for a second or two.

For such a little amount of liquid the contents of that tiny vial had a lot to give.

Just think, for a minute, of the sun—how really small it is as compared with our great universe—the solar system,—yet it gives light and heat, to billions of people and to an uncharted vastness of space—and it keeps on giving and giving and giving.

When God saw how selfish people were becoming He sent Jesus to the world to teach us how to live.

Jesus was always thinking of other people and doing things for them. Never considering what might happen to him or his own comfort, but giving his services and his counsel to people in need of help. And even though people tried to destroy him his influence has remained to make life a bit easier for those who come in contact with him in prayer. Though the vial may be broken, the sweetness of his life remains and will beautify the world.

"*. . . freely give.*"—MATTHEW 10:8.

A PRAYER

Dear God our Father, help us to live each day so that we shall deserve thy blessing. Keep us faithful to the ideals that Jesus has set for us. Grant that we may always act in the right way so that our homes will be always happy. Keep us from speaking too quickly lest we hurt the feelings of others who live with us.

Bless our parents and give them real joy in our home, and help us to be unselfish and contented. Amen.

A Message from Our Bible

"And as ye go, preach, saying, The kingdom of heaven is at hand.

Heal the sick, cleanse the lepers, raise the dead, cast out devils; freely ye have received, freely give.

Provide neither gold, nor silver, nor brass in your purses;

Nor scrip for your journey, neither two coats, neither shoes, nor yet staves; for the workman is worthy of his meat."—Matthew 10:7–10.

45

PHONOGRAPHS

THERE are many ways by which the words we speak may be revealed to a great many people. There is the newspaper. There are books. The telephone and radio. By these many sources people are informed of what is going on in the world, and many find their entertainment in these ways.

Then there is the phonograph record player. Mr. Thomas Edison invented this machine many years ago. The music of a band or orchestra is recorded on a disc, and this disc is then placed on the machine and the music is played back.

While broadcasting from my church one Sunday a tape recording was made of the entire service. Wishing to hear how it all sounded from the audience I had it played back to me on a phonograph-like machine. Whether I liked it or not, I heard my voice and words just as I gave them over the air. I would like to have made some changes—but it was too late!

I was thinking how you and I are combination records and phonographs. Words that other people speak make an impression upon us and so we often go right out and reproduce,—repeat—them to someone else. I hope that whatever recordings you allow to impress you are helpful, and true, and good. If a lie is impressed upon you, whispered to you on the quiet, throw that record out of your thoughts and never repeat it,—for once you have repeated it you cannot easily change it!

I believe God speaks to us quietly, and if in prayer and worship we let him make an impression upon us, let us go out and reproduce his words and wishes as Jesus did. Like the phonograph let us be reproducers, revealing the voice of God.

". . . God shall reveal this unto you."—PHILIPPIANS 3:15.

A PRAYER

Dear Jesus, we thank thee for the many stories thou hast told, which show us the love of God so well. Help us to heed thy counsel and so live that we may be a good influence to other children.

Keep us from doing things or speaking words that will hurt anyone. Give us courage to refuse to listen to lies or gossip, and may we never, never repeat evil words that come to our ears.

Give us thy strength that we may help others according to thy teachings. Amen.

A Message from Our Bible

"I press toward the mark for the prize of the high calling of God in Christ Jesus.

Let us therefore, as many as be perfect, be thus minded: and if in any thing ye be otherwise minded, God shall reveal even this unto you.

Nevertheless, whereto we have already attained, let us walk by the same rule, let us mind the same thing.

For our conversation is in heaven; from whence also we look for the Saviour, the Lord Jesus Christ."—Philippians 3:14–16, 20.

46

PLOWING WATER

Up and down a large field I used to walk behind a plow —back and forth, back and forth. One furrow turned over didn't seem to amount to much but after a day's work I would look back and then I could see that a lot of the ground had been plowed and I really had accomplished something.

People like to see some results of the work they do. For a week or so during November, men will go out deer hunting—but there isn't much sense in going unless there is snow on the ground! The hunter travels many miles until he runs across a deer track and then he follows it mile after mile and sometimes he catches up with his prey.

In almost everything we do we leave tracks for other folks to follow if they choose—tracks that lead to happy and safe results.

Sometimes, however, even real often, you see opportunities to help someone—an old person to cross a busy street; letting an older woman have your seat in the bus; saying "I'm sorry" even though you are not wholly at fault; sending warm clothes to Korea for children who are cold—doing kind deeds, without expecting rewards or recognition. It's like Plowing Water.

I watched many boats leave their docks and sail out to sea, after a few minutes there was no trail left behind where the boat plowed through the water! No boat could follow its track—neither could it retrace its path. But it reached its destination safely and returned with its cargo.

So it is, God expects us to do a lot of nice things in this world without being repaid in any way, without being recognized or honored. Our reward is the knowledge that we *did* them and that God is pleased.

"When thou doest alms, let not thy left hand know what thy right hand doeth."—Matthew 6:3.

A PRAYER

OUR Father, please make this world right and make people stop fighting each other. We know it is all our fault. We haven't always followed thy teaching, and there are so many who do not even know about thee. Help us be missionaries for thee and tell thy gospel to those who are heedless, that they may know of thy love for us all.

In unselfish service for thee we find our greatest happiness. Keep us faithful, O God, and so we pray for thy strength to help us. Amen.

A MESSAGE FROM OUR BIBLE

"Take heed that ye do not your alms before men, to be seen of them otherwise ye have no reward of your Father which is in heaven.

Therefore when thou doest thine alms do not sound a trumpet before thee, as the hypocrites do in the synagogues and in the streets, that they may have glory of men. Verily I say unto you, They have their reward.

But when thou doest alms, let not thy left hand know what thy right hand doeth;

That thine alms may be in secret; and thy Father which seeth in secret himself shall reward thee openly."—MATTHEW 6:1–4.

47

POLISH

DID you ever watch your father polish his car? Or a table top? Or the floor? First it has to be thoroughly cleaned. Every bit of dirt and grease should be removed! Then, with dry soft cloths, he wipes it until it is perfectly dry. Now it is already to receive a polish, so Dad gets a clean, soft cloth and a can or bottle of good polish and puts it on, rubbing it gently until it all seems to disappear. When the car is all done you all stand back and admire it. How it shines!

Now take some of that polish and put it on the tires! Nothing much happens. The tires may look a bit cleaner but that's all. They don't shine as the car body does! I wonder why! Polish seems to be wasted when put on the tires.

Well, of course, the reason is that polish looks best on anything, when there is beauty beneath the surface.

When there is no particular beauty to a surface, like the side of a house, or garage, or a bookcase, or the walls of a room,—paint is put on to cover up knots, and blemishes, and stains that have gotten into the grain of the wood in some manner.

Sometimes articles are painted that should have been polished. We have a stand at home for which we paid twenty-five cents. It was covered with paint. An expert removed the paint and found a very beautiful inlay table, for which we have been offered fifty dollars!

When Jesus saw people doing wrong he looked underneath their painted coat of evil and saw the good in them—and polished them with his love until their better nature shone through. Always remember that what you do or say is the paint or polish that emphasizes your character, that tells the world what is in your heart.

"Father, forgive them, for they know not what they do."—LUKE 23:34.

A PRAYER

Dear God, help us to be worthy of thy trust in us, and may we live up to what our parents would like to have us be.

Thank thee for a happy day. There are so many things that are right and good, teach us to be happy in disposition and contented with what we have.

Bless all boys and girls and help them do right. For Jesus' sake we ask. Amen.

A Message from Our Bible

"And when they were come to the place, which is called Calvary, here they crucified him, and the malefactors, one on the right hand, and the other on the left.

Then said Jesus, Father, forgive them; for they know not what they do. And they parted his raiments, and cast lots."—Luke 23:33–34.

48

PUMPS

You all know what a bicycle pump is I'm sure, or an automobile tire pump. In order to push air into the tire you first have to fill your pump with air.

I wonder if you ever saw, or used, a water pump. A pipe is driven deep into the ground and on top of it is this pump which draws the water up to the surface and deposits it in a tub or pail.

Now, in order to get that water into the pail, the pump has to be first filled with water!

In our farm house there is a pump in the kitchen. It has not been in use for many years. However, I recall when I was a boy, working the handle of that pump and filling tubs and pails with lovely clear water. On winter nights we would always let the water out of the pump else it would freeze in the cold kitchen. Then each morning someone would "start" the pump by pouring a cupful or a quart of water into it and rapidly pumping the handle, up and down, and pretty soon the cold water would come. This was called priming the pump.

What I want you to understand by this parable is that it took water to get water! Just a little water in the pump would allow it to draw up enough drinking water for all day. Prime the pump with water and you get water—or with air and you get a lot of air to force into your balloon.

I think Jesus must have used pumps of some kind,— for he certainly knew that if you "give, it shall be given unto you—good measure, pressed down, running over." He knew, because he lived that way—always giving, and because of him the love of God has flowed into all the world.

It surely depends upon you and me giving our little bit, if God's love is ever going to supply the world with happiness.

"Give and it shall be given unto you."—Luke 6:38.

A PRAYER

Dear God, our Father, we thank thee that the supply of thy great love is unlimited, and that it will be supplied to all who are ready and willing.

Teach us to do our part in being worthy of thy friendship by being friendly and inviting others to share our blessings.

Teach us to be worthy of thy sacrifice, by giving a portion of what we have to the advancement of thy Kingdom through our Church.

Teach us to be worthy of thy great love by showing kindness toward the unfortunate, by expressions of love toward people whom it would be easy to dislike or even hate.

Teach us the sure truth that "It is better to give than to receive" for we know full well that other truth "Give and it shall be given unto you . . . seven fold, pressed down, running over." Amen.

A Message from Our Bible

"As ye would that men should do to you do ye also to them likewise.

For if ye love them which love you, what thank have you? for sinners also love those that love them.

Give, and it shall be given unto you; good measure, pressed down, and shaken together, and running over, shall men give into your bosom. For with the same measure that ye mete withal it shall be measured to you again."—Luke 6:31, 32, 38.

49

RICE

WHEN you think of Rice the name of what country comes to your mind? China! Sure. We seem to have the idea that rice grows only in China, but believe it or not rice is becoming one of our important American crops. We naturally think of China because, for many centuries, that country has depended on Rice.

When you see your mother measure out half a cupful of rice it doesn't look like much for a hungry boy or girl as she pours it into a double boiler with a little water—but at lunch time that dish is full!

Just for a test, one time, I put a spoonful of rice in a small cardboard box and added a spoonful of water. I then closed the box tightly and awaited the result. In just a few hours I looked at my box of rice and found it had broken open and rice was oozing out all around it!

Even though we do raise some rice in our country, the Chinese export a lot of it to us and to all nations.

I read of a freighter in distress during a storm in the Pacific. Their SOS was heard and rescue was not too far away. The freighter was not taking water fast and there was no danger of water causing her to sink. However, down deep in the hold the entire crew was working feverishly shoveling the cargo of wet rice into the sea. You see, the danger was not in the storm but in the swelling of the wet rice. If the men hadn't shoveled it out, the rice would have filled the hold and burst open the sides of the old freighter.

Just as a little rice will feed and nourish a multitude of people, so it is that a little kindness will reach out and give a lot of cheer to many people. A little love multiplies a hundred fold when expressed in terms of unselfishness. Just because of you, many people will know happiness, and because of Jesus the world will find peace.

"If God so loved us, we ought also to love one another."—I JOHN 4:11.

A PRAYER

OPEN our hearts, dear Lord, that we may see the needs and the hardships in our world as well as the many many joys. May our thoughts be open to thy love that it may, daily, be expressed through us.

Bless the young folks in all lands, and give them a feeling of security and grant that they may seriously and stedfastly follow thy way of life.

Give aid to our missionaries in all parts of the world, O God, and grant that peace may crown their activities, through the love of Jesus. Amen.

A MESSAGE FROM OUR BIBLE

"Beloved, let us love one another; for love is of God; and every one that loveth is born of God, and knoweth God.

He that loveth not knoweth not God, for God is love.

If God so loved us, we ought also to love one another. Hereby know we that we dwell in him, and he in us, because he hath given us of his Spirit.

We love him because he first loved us.

And this commandment have we from him, That he who loveth God love his brother also."—I JOHN 4:7, 8, 11, 13, 19–20.

50

RIVER ROADS AND HIGH ROADS

As, OF course, you know, a river cuts its own path. It begins as a small spring up in the hills. It becomes too full and runs over and as that tiny stream trickles down over the rocks it is joined by other streams and as it reaches the valley it has cut a deep path for itself.

As you take long rides over secondary roads in the country you will note that a great number of them follow along beside a river. This is also quite true of railroad tracks.

Now, these roads were not laid out along the rivers because they needed water or because of the scenery, but merely because it was easier to build them on low land.

Some time ago the road engineers decided they wouldn't build a railroad all the way around Hoosac Mountain in Massachusetts, so men started to drill through the mountain. I was greatly interested when I learned that they started at both ends of the proposed tunnel which would be about two miles long.

Believe it or not, when they met in the center they were less than one-quarter of an inch out of line!

The floods of rivers wash away river roads but no floods reach into this tunnel.

Most roads, now are constructed away from rivers—high above their banks and through mountains.

God never meant us to build river roads for our lives where floods of evil and greed enter in and wash away the foundation of our Christian training.

He gave us mountains to cut through, and hills to go over—He meant us to build high roads.

"Who shall ascend into the hill of the Lord?"—PSALM 24:3.

A PRAYER

Dear Lord, help us live each day as thou hast taught us in the life of thy son Jesus Christ.

Help us to be useful each day as we mingle with each other at home or at school.

Keep us sincere in all we do and say, that people will learn to trust us, and make us worthy of thy love.

We thank thee for home and church and the influence they have toward peace on earth as we all reflect the love of Jesus Christ our Lord.   Amen.

A Message from Our Bible

"Who shall ascend into the hill of the Lord?   And who shall stand in his holy place?

He that hath clean hands, and a pure heart; Who hath not lifted up his soul unto falsehood, And hath not sworn deceitfully.

He shall receive a blessing from the Lord, And righteousness from the God of his salvation."—Psalm 24: 3-5.

ROCKS

THERE is something about a rock that gives us a sense of security. When a man wants to build a house he doesn't look for an easy sand pit for its foundation to rest on. He finds solid earth and then mixes rocks with the cement for his house to set on!

Any boy will tell us that when he sees a big rock out in some field or pasture he wants to climb on top of it, and he feels he is the master of all he sees.

It's a wonderful feeling when you are swimming in a mud bottom lake and you are so tired you think you can't reach shore, you suddenly feel your feet hit a solid rock and you can stand up and rest.

Several years ago I saw that very large rock out in the middle of San Francisco Bay. On it are some very strong buildings to take care of people who do wrong and have to be kept away from others because they are dangerous. This rock of protection is called Alcatraz.

But I prefer to think about Plymouth Rock on which the Pilgrims stepped from the *Mayflower*. For many days only water was under them to hold them up and now at last a Rock, and they felt very safe.

I trust that America will always give people the feeling of safety.

Jesus spoke of a Rock when he referred to one of his disciples as the kind of a person he could organize his church around. This disciple, Peter, proved to be dependable, trustworthy, honest, fearless, and strong. That's the way Christ wants his church to be. Won't you try to be those solid foundations for God right where you live so that his church will grow and thrive until all the world is truly Christian?

"*. . . upon this rock I will build my church. . . .*"
—MATTHEW 16:18.

A PRAYER

WE LOOK to thee, Our Father, with humble hearts as we recognize thy great love and thoughtfulness toward us.

We have been wrong in many ways but in repentance we are sure of thy forgiveness. Thy patience with us is everlasting and thy love enduring.

We thank thee for giving to us thy Son, and for his unselfish way of life. Grant that his example may set within us a desire and drive to establish thy will and plan upon this earth.

Help the young folks to see clearly how to build their lives upon the foundation of the Christian religion. May the teachings of Jesus as he saw some of them in Peter, be the foundation structure of our lives in our attitude and deeds.

Bless our homes and our Church and give us all a sense of deep responsibility and help us recognize the right as against the wrong. Amen.

A MESSAGE FROM OUR BIBLE

". . . Whom do men say that I, the Son of man, am?

And they said, Some say that thou art John the Baptist; some, Elias; and others, Jeremias, or one of the prophets.

He saith unto them, But whom say ye that I am?

And Simon Peter answered and said, Thou art the Christ, the Son of the living God.

And Jesus answered and said unto him, Blessed art thou, Simon Bar-jona; For flesh and blood hath not revealed it unto thee, but my Father which is in heaven."
MATTHEW 16:13–17.

52

ROPES

"Hanging by a thread." Did you ever hear that expression? Maybe it's a button on your coat, so you sew it on. (I'm sure you can do it without bothering mother.) I've seen spiders hanging down from a tree branch or a shed roof, "by a thread!"—How tiny that thread is! But weave a million of them together and you have a rope. A spider's web is very strong because there are so many of those tiny silken threads woven into a pattern.

Several years ago while serving a church in Lowell, Massachusetts, the Steeple, the highest in the city, was receiving new slate shingles. I used to watch the Steeple Jack as, with only a rope he walked up and around that steeple at its dizzy height. Each day he inspected the rope and always used a new rope when he started a new job. One tiny broken strand would be a warning and a danger signal.

We sometimes think, just because we are only one person, that what we do won't make any difference,—but we are like that pebble thrown into a lake; it causes a ripple and each ripple causes another and another until the whole lake is disturbed. One person making a disturbance in a class affects the whole class and the teacher.

Some boys and girls, and older people too, like to have their own way all the time. Football teams would be pretty weak if each boy thought of, and considered, only himself without cooperating with the moves of the other ten!

Jesus taught us how to live and work together by the spirit of love and consideration toward each other, woven together into a strong church.

". . . *That their hearts may be encouraged as they are knit together in love. . . .*"—COLOSSIANS 2:2.

A PRAYER

DEAR God, our Father, there is so much to be thankful for in this beautiful world,—please make us worthy of all thy gifts. So often, we complain and find fault of what others do, heedless of our own mistakes.

Help us see the goodness in others and make us always ready to cooperate in any attempt to carry thy gospel wherever it is most needed.

Keep us trustworthy and always ready to do as thou desire as revealed in Jesus Christ our Lord. Amen.

A MESSAGE FROM OUR BIBLE

"For I want you to know how greatly I strive for you, —and for all who have not seen my face, that their hearts may be encouraged as they are knit together in love, to have all the riches of assured understanding and the knowledge of God's mystery, of Christ, in whom are hid all the treasures of wisdom and knowledge.

As therefore you received Christ Jesus the Lord, so live in him: rooted and built up in him and established in the faith, just as you were taught, abounding in thanksgiving."—COLOSSIANS 2:1–3, 6, 7.

53
SALT

I LIKE that old hymn "Count Your Blessings"; it makes me want to sit down and count the many many natural resources we have in America to make us healthy.

I drove across the salt flats in Utah several years ago and all one could see was that vast whiteness of salt many feet deep. And the Great Salt Lake beach is of salt instead of sand!

There are places on earth where there is no salt and people live only because they eat raw meat of animals which have found "salt licks" in the jungle where animals, which ordinarily would kill each other, have been seen together!

Men, however, have fought many battles to gain control of a small salt field.

I have read, that during Napoleon's retreat from Moscow, the lack of salt caused the death of thousands of his men, for wounds will not heal without salt.

The ancient Roman soldiers were given salt as a part of their equipment—or a special amount of money called his salarium by which he would buy salt. Our word "salary" comes from this word "salarium."

There is salt enough in America and in other countries to supply the whole world's needs, and yet some people are really suffering because certain others put a high price on it and some governments have taxed it.

There are so many people in our world today who need Christianity, yet, just because it costs us a few dollars to send missionaries to these needy people they say "why bother."

Salt may keep people alive but Christianity makes them happy and gives them new hope and teaches them to live in peace and love with each other.

"Go ye into all the world, and preach the Gospel to every creature."—MARK 16:15.

A PRAYER

Dear God, have patience with me. I get so angry sometimes at such little things only to find many times that I am wrong.

Teach me to do the right as thou hast taught.

Teach me, dear Lord, to be more thoughtful and lead me to do the right as thou hast taught me.

Bless my home and church, dear God, that their influence in the community may be felt always for good, and grant that I may grow to be more like thee as I strive to do thy will. Amen.

A Message from Our Bible

"Afterward he appeared unto the eleven as they sat at meat, and upbraided them with their unbelief and hardness of heart, because they believed not them which had seen him after he was risen.

And he said unto them, Go ye into all the world, and preach the gospel to every creature.

He that believeth and is baptized shall be saved; but he that believeth not shall be damned.

And they went forth, and preached every where, the Lord working with them, and confirming the word with signs following."—Mark 16:14–16, 20.

54

SHADOWS

ORDINARILY, when I see a shadow, I know there is a boy or a girl, or tree or an elephant standing close by.

Of course, the size of the shadow depends upon the strength of the light that is behind it or above it. A tree casts a much longer shadow at near sundown than at noon! Did you ever see a play in pantomime? The figures on the screen are large or small depending on how near the light is to the object being shown.

While riding along a country road late one afternoon my eyes caught the shadows of telephone poles and noticing one was crooked it attracted my attention and looking at the pole, sure enough, it was crooked—broken in three places where it had been hit by some car, I suppose.

You see if things or people stand in a bright light they cast shadows just as they are. It seems to me that a lie is a crooked shadow—and if that is so, then the person who makes that shadow must be crooked in his ideals. If a boy cheats in whatever game he is playing, it shows he is not quite straightforward in his character, for the wrong deed he does reveals a crooked thought.

Then I looked out of my window and saw some fluttering shadows—shadows that wavered back and forth as though the wind was blowing them around. Sure enough up on the roof someone had hung out some sheets and they were drying in the breeze.

Sometimes some people are like that, you can't quite trust them. They say one thing to you and tell you how grand you are, and then criticize you to other people!

I like people who are straightforward and honest— people who will cast straight, and not crooked shadows.

"He that walketh uprightly, walketh surely."—PROVERBS 10:9.

A PRAYER

DEAR God, our loving Father, help us to be worthy of thy trust in us. Show us how we may practice every day, the teaching of thy great love. Teach us how to live as Jesus lived.

Keep us from being critical of others and give us willing hearts that we may be considerate of the needs of people all over the world.

Help us bring peace to the world of Nations, by having it in our own hearts and being willing to exemplify it right where we are in our homes, our community and nation.

Save the children of all nations from starvation; from bitterness; and grant that they may find joy in the gospel of Jesus that we as Church people carry to them. Inspire us, dear Lord, with earnestness and the will to help. In the name of Jesus. Amen.

A MESSAGE FROM OUR BIBLE

"A wise son maketh a glad father; But a foolish son is the heaviness to his mother.

The Lord will not suffer the soul of the righteous to famish.

Blessings are upon the head of the righteous; But violence covereth the mouth of the wicked.

The wise heart will receive commandments; But a prating fool shall fall.

He that walketh uprightly walketh surely; But he that perverteth his ways shall be known."—PROVERBS 10:1, 6, 8, 10.

55

SHARE THE TREE

SOME time ago I recall hearing over a radio news broadcast of an interesting incident that happened in a hollow tree.

It seemed that this hollow tree was the home of a large family of squirrels! They were very happy and quite contented because they had worked hard storing up nuts for the winter and now it was late fall and they were settling down to a warm comfortable winter, when a swarm of bees, seeing this hollow tree, decided to take over.

Now, the bees didn't know the squirrels were there until they began to leave one by one—and fast!

Thousands and thousands of bees poured in and the poor heartbroken squirrels just stood at a distance away thinking about all those nuts and the warmth of their abandoned home.

The bees got nicely settled in their new home and in doing so they thought of these poor dispossessed squirrels out in the cold wind. So the Queen sent out a messenger who motioned to the squirrels to come in.

Cautiously the squirrels approached the tree and finally looked inside and what do you think! The bees had appropriated only a part of the hollow tree and had left plenty of room for the squirrels. So, in they went, and it was observed that the squirrels would have honey on their nuts that winter!

Wouldn't it be nice if every nation and every race in the world would try to get along with each other better. If all had the Christian spirit of sharing instead of grasping, I'm sure the people of the world would be happy with each other and peace would be the result. Let's not try to appropriate the whole "tree."

———

"*. . . live peaceable with all.*"—ROMANS 12:18.

A PRAYER

WE LOOK to thee, O God, for counsel. Help us to realize that thou art always near, ready to help, reaching out thy helping hand toward us.

We look to thee for encouragement. When our problems seem big to us give us a portion of thy strength that we may find solutions that will leave us contented and wiser.

We look to thee for guidance in this world of thoughtlessness and jealousy and greed. Lead us away from such things. Help us to see values above the sordid material desires of so many people today.

We thank thee for thy love and care as expressed by Jesus. Make us truly thy children and help us live together in peace among the nations of the world. Amen.

A MESSAGE FROM OUR BIBLE

"Let love be without dissimulation. Abhor that which is evil; cleave to that which is good.

Be kindly affectioned one to another with brotherly love; in honor preferring one another;

Not slothful in business; fervent in spirit; serving the Lord.

Rejoicing in hope; patient in tribulation; continuing instant in prayer."—ROMANS 12:9–12.

56

SKYSCRAPERS AND STEEPLES

USUALLY, as I drive up to a church, I find the doors all securely locked, and no one is around to let me in, so I see only the outside of that beautiful building dedicated to God for the service of people. The steeple says "Come" but when I arrive I find no way of getting anywhere near it.

It often seems to say—"look at me. I rise above everything else, I am important."

And so it is important but not because of its size.

I stood one day, not long ago, looking down Wall Street,—that canyon of skyscrapers in New York City, and saw at the head of the street a steeple rising from a beautiful church to about the 12th story of twenty-story skyscrapers on either side.

It was a beautiful picture.

How crowded the street was with thousands and thousands of business men and women going to work to earn money to build more skyscrapers so that more money could be made by more people. The doors of the skyscrapers swung both ways. Elevators hummed. Crowds swarmed in and out.

But at the head of that financial district stands the church beckoning people to stop their rushing, and pause for prayer;—to cease their greedy desires and give to the needy—to do away with false gods and kneel before God the Father—to turn from selfish ways to the way of Jesus.

Skyscrapers beckon the crowds with the words "What can I do for you?" The steeple seems to say, "Come unto me all ye who are weary and heavy burdened and find rest to your souls."

"I was glad when they said unto me, Let us go into the house of the Lord."—PSALM 122:1.

A PRAYER

Dear Lord, we thank thee for our church, with the opportunities we have for worship. Give us the ability to help give thy gospel message to all the world through our enthusiasm and work.

Teach us to worship, that we may be filled with thy truth, and give the strength we need to live as thou would want us to.

Bless our leaders and all who give much of their time to teaching thy love and plan through action.

We pray for the missionaries who carry thy message to people who do not know of thee, to the sick and to the starving children of backward nations.

Help them, O God, and may we in Christian love do much to bring comfort to them. Bless our homes, dear Lord, and show us the right way in our every day actions, that we may always be at peace with each other. Amen.

A Message from Our Bible

"I was glad when they said unto me, Let us go into the house of the Lord.

Our feet are standing within thy gates, O Jerusalem,
For there are set thrones of judgment, The thrones of the house of David.

Pray for the peace of Jerusalem: They shall prosper that love thee.

Peace be within thy walls, And prosperity within thy palaces."—Psalm 122:1–2, 5–7.

57
SPIDERS

IN MY book "105 Modern Parables" I have several stories about animals and insects including one about "The Spider."

I love to watch spiders. Their motto seems to be ". . . try, try again!" If their web is upset they start right in rebuilding. I've seen a whole lawn full of these webs in the early morning when the dew is on the grass which shows them up very clearly. By night every web is destroyed but the next morning they have all been rebuilt!

One of the most interesting of the Spider family is the Water Spider. Because of him man can go down to the ocean bottom and examine wrecks of ships or study sea life! The invention of the Diving Bell—or suit—was inspired by watching a Water Spider come to the surface and take a bubble of air for ventilation and then go down into the water.

Do you recall the story when God sent a plague of flies upon Egypt? In order to do this He must have killed off all the Spiders or caused them to sleep, otherwise they would have destroyed the flies.

Sometime when you have a lot of leisure examine a spider's web! It is wonderfully made. Try to make one out of fine silk thread! Those silken threads are spun out of the spider's own body—it's a part of its very life, and if you sweep it down, the spider spins another right away. "Try, try again."

God seems to teach us wonderful lessons by everyone of the live and inanimate things He creates, and among the many lessons the spider teaches us there are two that stand out clearly. In building our character and in doing our work let us put the very best of ourselves into the effort.

Be *"patient in tribulation; continuing stedfastly in prayer."*—ROMANS 12:12.

A PRAYER

MANY times we disappoint thee, O God, we know, and fall far short of being our best selves. Forgive us we pray and lead us to try again and again.

Deep down in our hearts we want to do right, and say the kind words that make for happiness; but there are times when we speak too sharply and act too quickly.

Give us wisdom to think clearly and the ability to carry out thy plan of peace for this world in the way Jesus demonstrated for us. Amen.

A MESSAGE FROM OUR BIBLE

"Be kindly affectioned one to another with brother love; in honour preferring one another.

Not slothful in business; fervent in spirit; serving the Lord.

Rejoicing in hope; patient in tribulation; continuing instant in prayer.

Distributing to the necessity of saints; given to hospitality.

Bless them which persecute you; bless, and curse not."
—ROMANS 12:10–14.

58

STANDARD GAUGE

ONE of the many things I used to like to do when a boy, was to run out to the cliff in front of our house and look down onto the railroad tracks and watch the powerful engines drawing a long line of loaded cars along those rails. As I would sit waiting for a train I would wonder about those rails. They seemed to be very heavy, as, indeed, they had to be, to stand the weight of those trains.

Of course, the rails had to be spiked exactly the same distance apart or the train as it went along, would come off the tracks and cause a wreck and people might be hurt. This distance between the rails is called the gauge.

As different Railroads pioneered into many towns and cities and states the gauge was varied, so that the trains over one line could not travel over any other. After several years when train travel became more popular all railroads were laid down by the same gauge and became the Standard for all roads so as to allow trains to use each other's lines. This Standard Gauge is four feet, eight and one half inches.

I suppose a yardstick would be called a gauge because it's a standard of measurement.

What about your life and your decision as to what is right and what is wrong? What is your Standard Gauge?

When I see some people just walking on the sidewalk I feel that they are Christians. They seem to radiate happiness and thoughtfulness of others and the love of service. I sense that Jesus is their example of living.

Let Jesus be your Standard Gauge, always, in your words and deeds.

———

"Jesus Christ the same yesterday, and today, and for ever."—HEBREWS 13:8.

A PRAYER

WE THANK thee, dear Lord, for a happy day, and for our friends with whom we have played. Bless our parents who have watched over us and grant that thy loving care may be appreciated by all.

As we sleep tonight, watch over us and give us peaceful rest, that when morning comes we may be ready to face new duties and problems, and be prepared to enjoy another day of happy service. Amen.

A MESSAGE FROM OUR BIBLE

". . . the Lord is my helper, and I will not fear what man shall do unto me.

Remember them which have the rule over you, who have spoken unto you the word of God; whose faith follow, considering the end of their conversation.

Jesus Christ the same yesterday, and today, and for ever."—HEBREWS 13:6–8.

59

STARS

IF I SHOULD tell you that you never see any Stars, I expect it would be hard for you to believe it. You see our sun and moon and the planets—but those fixed Stars up over your heads you do not see, at least with the naked eyes!

How far can you see with your naked eyes? Along the earth's surface, one sees about four miles. Looking into space you might see ten miles or twenty,—or perhaps even fifty miles,—but the stars you think you see are not the stars at all, but the light which left the stars at least four years ago, and in the case of many, the lights you see left the stars before Christ was born.

You can't see the stars. You can only see the light which the stars have given out. And even though the star may have been extinguished a hundred years ago, still its light shines on.

In connection with this parable it occurs to me that, when you meet a car, on a dark night, you cannot see it because of its headlights!

When someone holds a flash-light in front of him and "spots it" on you, all you can see distinctly is the light—but you know there is a person behind it!

We do not actually see God at any time, but we vision him every day in beauty, kindness, in love, and—in fact, in all of Jesus' teachings. All these tell us of God.

Jesus was the Light from God, revealing him to us. The Christmas spirit of love, and good cheer tells us of God.

Everything good we see, we know comes from him and so we know God, and that truly, he is Love, and we too as his helpers are more lights, by which others may better understand God.

"That was the true light that lighteth every man."— JOHN 1:9.

A PRAYER

THOU, O Christ, art the Light of the world.

Help us to live in that light and grant that we may be so filled with it that it will radiate thy blessing to young folks who need the warmth of thy loving care.

Teach us how to carry the light of thy gospel message into dark areas where people are spiritually weak and mentally discouraged.

Use us, O God, as friends of Jesus, to impart thy will to those who are weak, or ill, or shut in, and may our prayers for strength be answered as we seek thy peace and love, through Jesus Christ our Lord.   Amen.

A MESSAGE FROM OUR BIBLE

"There was a man sent from God, whose name was John.

The same came for a witness, to bear witness of the Light, that all men through him might believe.

He was not that Light, but was sent to bear witness of the Light.

That was the true Light, which lighteth every man that cometh into the world."—JOHN 1 :6–9.

60

STEAM

I BELIEVE I told you once, in one of my parables, about a tiny tree I saw take root in the crevice of a great rock. The roots found soil in that crack and began to grow. After a few years the tree and the roots were so big that the solid rock split apart. Those tiny roots, growing, did to that rock what man could have done only with dynamite.

There is tremendous power in nature.

Now, if you confine water in a covered dish and then boil it, something has to break loose, the steam which nature manufactures in those tiny bubbles just has to get out, so, if there is no other way the dish will blow up!

You can't see that steam when you pour the cold water into the dish, neither can you see the steam at any time—for steam is the power that expands the water. Steam is action and the greater the fire is, under it, the more powerful is that action. By it engines are run; furnaces give out heat, and food is cooked.

Now, my young friends, don't you find it much easier to do the things you dislike to tackle, or to run errands, when you make a kind of game of the tasks—such as timing yourself or competing with your sister or brother? A little enthusiasm in doing your work is like the fire under the water, producing steam power.

Christianity is like steam. You can't see it, but if you will exercise it in your life, build a fire of enthusiasm under it, and put it into action, it will produce *results*.

Really use your Christianity all the time, and it will work powerfully for you.

———

"What is truth?"—JOHN 18:38.

A PRAYER

MOST merciful and loving God, we thank thee for the Power thou dost bestow upon each one of us, to be used for our growth and service.

We are strong only as we use the strength of thy love and kindness lodged in our hearts.

Help us be worthy of possessing thy spirit within us, and inspire us to use thee in our relations with one another, and in the world of hard work.

Guide us, O God, in the conduct of our government affairs, that our leaders may be honest and trustworthy as they plan the future of our nation and world. Inspire us with thy presence, O Lord, and walk life's way with us and teach us to pray with the fervor and faith of our Lord and Saviour. Amen.

A MESSAGE FROM OUR BIBLE

"Then Pilate—said unto him, Art thou the King of the Jews?

. . . thine own nation and the chief priests have delivered thee unto me; what hast thou done?

Jesus answered My Kingdom is not of this world; if my kingdom were of this world, then would my servants fight, that I should not be delivered to the Jews; but now is my kingdom not from hence.

. . . thou sayest that I am a king. To this end was I born, and for this cause came I into the world, that I should bear witness unto the truth. Every one that is of the truth heareth my voice.—JOHN 18:33, 35–37.

61

THE WAY OF A STREAM

A STREAM of water running down over rocks and dropping over cliffs and forming whirlpools is most attractive to the average boy—and girl. But you seldom see a stream running straight. It follows the way of least resistance. If you follow a stream along a meadow or side hill you will often travel the distance of two miles to reach a point only half a mile away!

Sometimes you will follow a stream for miles and miles, as I did in New Mexico, only to suddenly realize it has completely disappeared! This was the Hombolt River that just drops out of sight in the sand.

When you cross the street you wait for the green light and then walk straight to the other side. You don't run out into traffic and dodge in and out among the cars and trucks, I hope!

The way of a stream is crooked. It doesn't wait for a green light for a straight course. It sees a rock and goes around it. It sees a hill and goes around it. It comes to a log and changes its course. It comes to a hollow place and just stays there for a while! It follows the way of least resistance.

Could that be the reason why some young folks do wrong things—and say bad words?

They see and hear others and just follow their example. It's easier than using your own brains and kicking obstacles out of your path.

God has shown us in the teachings of Jesus how to travel a straight course,—how to overcome obstacles and temptations. Look carefully at every question of right and wrong and determine to take the straight course, even though it's more difficult.

" . . . *by the rivers of water.*"—PSALM I :3.

A PRAYER

WE THANK thee, dear Lord, for the privilege we have of coming to thy house—the Church, dedicated to thee and to thy service.

As we express our acknowledgment of thy great love, may we fulfill the purposes for which thou didst send thy Son, Jesus Christ. We thank thee for the goodness thou hast expressed again and again in forgiving our wrong acts.

Thou dost give us the strength to do thy will and to follow the teachings of thy Son Jesus Christ.

Often we fail and take the road of least resistance only to lose our way to thee and sink lower than we should in character.

Strengthen all who are weak and guide them in the right way as they make important decisions through Jesus Christ our Lord. Amen.

A MESSAGE FROM OUR BIBLE

"Blessed is the man that walketh not in the counsel of the wicked, Nor standeth in the way of sinners, Nor sitteth in the seat of the scoffers.

But his delight is in the law of the Lord; And on his law doth he meditate day and night.

And he shall be like a tree planted by the streams of water, That bringeth forth its fruit in its season, Whose leaf also doth not wither And whatsoever he doeth shall prosper."—PSALM 1 :1–3.

62

" .335 "

I EXPECT nearly all the boys know what I am going to talk about for this Parable message. Of course, ".335" might be the number of a house on some street,—or it could be a telephone number, I suppose, or a dog license.

However, if your eyes are sharp you have noticed a tiny dot in front of the figures,—and that gives it away to all who know anything about baseball. It's the best batting average listed among the Dodgers (the Brooklyn, N.Y., National League Club) at the close of their 1951 season and I'll bet most of you know to whom I'm referring—that's right,—Jackie Robinson; and he held third place for the whole country.

Now, a perfect batting average (1.000), as in everything we do, is not easy to attain, especially over a period of days and months! You see even Jackie can't hit that ball safely every time he is at the plate—if he did, how sad the opposing pitchers would be!

The excitement in every game comes in seeing how near to perfection each player and each team can come.

All of us, no doubt, would like to be one hundred per cent perfect in all we attempt but the fact remains we are not. However, the important thing is,—do we keep on trying?

For instance, I heard two boys arguing, each forcefully declaring he was right, whereas neither of them was one hundred per cent right. No doubt one of them may have been only about one third right, .335.

God knows that perfection is hard to attain. He sent Jesus to us to show that it's possible to reach it in character and so we keep on trying—coming up to the plate hopefully seeking a home run or an infield hit—lifting our batting average. We only hope for perfection as we try for it.

"Seek ye the Lord while he may be found; call upon Him while he is near."—ISAIAH 55 :6.

A PRAYER

DEAR Father of us all, help us to know right from wrong. We speak and act too quickly many times a day. Forgive us if we hurt people by what we say and by our thoughtless acts toward our parents, our brothers or sisters, and our friends.

Make us better than we are.

Help us be more like Jesus and so be good examples to everyone who plays with us.

Through us, dear Lord, cause our homes to be happy, and live with us every day, and watch over us each night. Amen.

A MESSAGE FROM OUR BIBLE

"Seek ye the Lord while he may be found, call ye upon him while he is near;

Let the wicked forsake his way, and the unrighteous man his thoughts and let him return unto the Lord, and he will have mercy upon him, and to our God for he will abundantly pardon.

. . . As the heavens are higher than the earth, so are my ways higher than your ways, and my thoughts than your thoughts.

For as the rain cometh down, and the snow from heaven,—and watereth the earth and maketh it to bring forth and bud, that it may give seed to the sower and bread to the eater;

So shall my word be that goeth forth out of my mouth; —it shall accomplish that which I please, and it shall prosper in the things whereto I sent it."—ISAIAH 55: 6–7, 9–11.

63

THUMBS

MOST people use their tongues when they talk! Many people also talk to their friends by writing. Some people even talk with their shoulders—especially when they say "I don't know" or "So what!" But almost all of us talk with our hands.

Hands can be very expressive, and for my parable today I want to ask you, when you get home, to stretch your arms out to the sides, and spread your fingers and thumbs wide open, palms front.

Now make believe your hand is the church or your home or perhaps the nation and the fingers represent the individual people in the church or home or nation pointing outward in service,—anxious to be of use, reaching to touch other lives with the teaching of Jesus.

Notice, as you look at your extended hands, that the thumbs point upward. This, of course, like the steeple of a church, reminds us of God, who is the most vital part of our church, home and country, for he touches every one of us by his love and care.

Just notice how important that thumb is. It is the only one of the five fingers on each hand that can touch the other four with equal pressure.

If you have any doubts about the importance of the thumb—try picking up a pin from the floor without using your thumb.

So, that most important thumb, reminding us of God, teaches us that if we want to be useful, and help build a better community and world, always remember to consider God in what we do and say.

"Go and make disciples of all nations."—MATTHEW 28:19.

A PRAYER

Dear God, our Father, we thank thee for thy love—expressed in so many ways.

As thy children, we know thou dost care for us. Teach us the way of thy life and help us follow according to thy way of faith and work.

Bless the young folks, dear Lord; may they be taught to worthily magnify thy name.

There is so much to do, to make this world according to thy plan. Thy Son Jesus has taught us the way. Grant that we may follow his lead making it ours in our daily walk of life.

Give thy comfort to those who are sick—or weary—or bereaved and to all who are sad. Amen.

A Message from Our Bible

"Then the eleven disciples went away into Galilee, into a mountain where Jesus had appointed them.

And when they saw him, they worshipped him; but some doubted. And Jesus came and spake unto them, saying, All power is given unto me in heaven and in earth.

Go ye therefore and teach all nations, baptizing them in the name of the Father, and of the Son, and of the Holy Ghost;

Teaching them to observe all things whatsoever I have commanded you; and lo, I am with you alway, even unto the end of the world."—Matthew 28 : 16–20.

64

THE TIDE

As I sat on a fishing wharf, not long ago, I noticed how black the posts were that supported the landings where many big boats were tied up.

Knowing that that blackness was caused by the water, I realized the tide was at its lowest and was starting to come in.

In six hours, if I had waited there that long, all these big fishing "draggers" and seiners would be lifted about twelve feet higher—for then it would be high tide.

Near the entrance to Gloucester Harbor, one of the busiest harbors on the New England coast, there is a rock rising out of the sea, a short distance from the shore known as "Norman's Woe." Perhaps you have read about it in school when you have been reading Longfellow's poems, for he names this rock when he tells about "The Wreck of the Hesperus." Anchored near this big rock is a buoy but the anchor chain is long enough so that this buoy is lifted as the tide rises and it always floats on the surface warning mariners to steer their boats away from "Norman's Woe."

Then there was that rock in the entrance channel to San Francisco Bay. Heavy cables were anchored to it and attached to a big scow on the ocean's surface at low tide. The rising tide lifted the rock and it was floated out to deep sea!

The lifting power of the tide is certainly tremendous. I hope it reminds you, as it does me, of the lifting power of God—of Christianity.

Jesus found his great strength in prayer. When you are unhappy, or angry at someone, thoughts of God will lift you to higher levels and keep you worthy of being an example to others and so steering them from wrong doing.

"Humble yourselves in the sight of the Lord, and he will lift you up."—JAMES 4:10.

A PRAYER

THOU, O God, who art perfect, lift us again and again nearer to thy perfection of character in our lives.

When we are low and we find ourselves grumbling, come into our minds and hearts and raise us to higher levels.

There is so much in the world that is wrong and so little we can seem to do, yet we know thy loving care and power is underneath us all and will lift us out of all wrong if we will place ourselves on thy love.

Grant that we may see thy truth always raised above the evils and sins, and give us strength to rise to its height. Amen.

A MESSAGE FROM OUR BIBLE

"Submit yourselves, therefore, to God. Resist the devil, and he will flee from you.

Draw nigh to God, and he will draw nigh to you, Cleanse your hands; and purify your hearts.

Humble yourselves in the sight of the Lord and he shall lift you up.

Speak not evil one of another."—JAMES 4 :7, 8, 10, 11.

65

TIME ON OUR HANDS

THERE is an old expression I often hear from people and sometimes it is appropriate for young folks as well as old,—It is this "Time hangs heavy on my hands."

When I see boys and girls just standing on the street corners I want to go right up to them and say "time is rushing right along, why don't you get busy and keep up with it?" If you know you have studying to do why don't you get at it before it's too late?

During the last war a soldier wrote me from Bingen, Germany, and in the letter he told me of the incident when he was walking guard. At the end of his period his relief didn't show up until one hour and a half late!

In checking their watches the soldier who came late noted that his watch was running all right but the hands had stopped. So he was late for his watch when he was supposed to relieve his buddy.

My friend concluded his letter with the words "That's often the way in the world—time moves right along but our hands stay still."

How much time do you waste trying to get out of doing something? You just stand there arguing trying to show how important it is that you should do something else instead of that which you have been asked to do. Or perhaps you just sulk—sitting back doing and saying nothing—just wasting time.

Time moves on but your hands remain still.

I hope you will all try from now on to do, right off, the things you are asked to do. Don't let time get ahead of you! See that your hands keep up with the time. Don't always be late and slow. Be up and doing—on time.

———

"What thy hand findeth to do,—do it with thy might."
—ECCLESIASTES 9:10.

A PRAYER

DEAR God, we thank thee that there is work to do; grant us the will to always want to do our share. Help us to keep from shirking or leaving undone those things which are left to us to do.

Fill us with enthusiasm for thy church and the obligations accepted by which thy gospel truth may be spread throughout the community.

Hear our simple prayers, O Lord, and keep us faithful to thy trust in us. Bless our homes and watch over all who are sick or unhappy, and give them peace,—through Jesus' name. Amen.

A MESSAGE FROM OUR BIBLE

"Praise ye the Lord.

Oh give thanks unto the Lord; for he is good; for his lovingkindness endureth for ever.

Who can utter the mighty acts of the Lord? Or show forth all his praise?

Blessed are they that keep judgment, and he that doeth righteousness at all times."—PSALM 106:1–3.

66

A TREE GROWS

SEVERAL years ago while I was minister of a church in Lowell, Massachusetts, I wanted to have some trees growing around our house. So, one fall, I went to my farm in New Hampshire and dug up a few small cedars. I left as much soil on the roots as would stay and wrapped them in burlap and carefully brought them to Lowell and set them out. Two or three of them survived and grew, and two or three died.

I did this for several years and then when I went to the church in St. Johnsbury, I did the same thing with somewhat better results as I discovered that the more soil I took with the roots of those tiny trees, the surer I was that they would grow in their new home.

I have been interested in the new parks being constructed here in our city and thousands of large trees are brought by trucks from some distance to be set out to beautify these various garden spots. However, one thing I have noticed particularly is the huge amount of soil which is brought on the roots of the trees. The more native soil brought with the tree the surer it is of taking root and growing in its new home.

People are like that too. They are happier, when they move from a town or city, if they have so lived as to take with them the friendship and respect of many people and especially the love of their home in the case of young people going to college or work.

Jesus came to this world and he could have been very lonely—but he wasn't, for he brought with him the love of God, and anyone who truly keeps that with him will always make new friends easily.

" . . . lo, I am with you even unto the end of the world."—MATTHEW 28:20.

A PRAYER

WE THANK thee, dear Lord, for faith.

Because of it, love and kindness and peace become more prominent in the world.

We thank thee for our faith in one another in our homes and within our circle of friends.

We thank thee for our faith in our country's leaders.

For faith in thee, O God, we are deeply grateful, for in our faith we find a power that keeps us from bitterness and discouragement.

Through our faith we become more trustful and so much happier. Keep us faithful, as Jesus was faithful with complete trust in thee. Amen.

A MESSAGE FROM OUR BIBLE

"Then the eleven disciples went away into Galilee, into a mountain where Jesus had appointed them.

And when they saw him, they worshipped him; but some doubted.

And Jesus came and spake unto them, saying, All power is given unto me in heaven and in earth.

Go ye therefore, and teach all nations, baptizing them in the name of the Father, and of the Son, and of the Holy Ghost;

Teaching them to observe all things whatsoever I have commanded you; and, lo, I am with you alway, even unto the end of the world."—MATTHEW 28:16–20.

67

TREE RINGS

A GREAT elm tree blew over during a hurricane some years ago and after it had been sawed off at the stump, in order to clear it away, I tried to count the tiny rings which one may see in every tree stump.

In building fences around a pasture, wires would often be stapled to trees. This would save driving posts, and trees would last much longer as they keep right on growing. After a few years the new growth would completely cover the wire—until after many years the wires seem to go right through the center of the tree!

The wires may retard the growth of the tree for a year or two—just as a stormy season or a dry summer will do, and this will cause the rings, for those years, to be much closer together.

So, as I counted the rings on that great elm tree stump, I could tell how many of the eighty-eight years were good, prosperous growing years, and how many were lean and dry seasons!

For every year's battle won against drought, tornadoes, killing frosts and hard winters there appeared a ring—like a band of triumph representing a year's growth.

Do things always go just as smoothly as you would like to have them? Don't always expect to have your own way! Brace yourself and accept disappointments, and cooperate with others, and you will be stronger in character and more useful as you grow into man- and womanhood. For every battle against temptation and hardship, you add a golden ring of character to your life, showing a definite growth as Jesus did in the preparation of his life. May God give you happy years of service that you may truly grow—

"until all attain . . . to the measure of the stature of the fulness of Christ."—EPHESIANS 4:13.

A PRAYER

Dear God, our Father, we thank thee for Jesus who came to this world and who taught us so much about life and its meaning and how it should be used.

May the inspiration of his kindness and generosity keep us from selfish desires, and build within us a spiritual growth which will show in our love and sacrifice for things worth while doing.

Help us, dear God, to please thee in what we say and in what we do—so shall we grow and be more worthy of thy great love and consideration. We pray not only for ourselves, but for all who need thy blessing. Amen.

A Message from Our Bible

"Till we all come in the unity of the faith, and of the knowledge of the Son of God, unto the perfect man, unto the measure of the stature of the fulness of Christ:

Speaking the truth in love, we may grow up into him in all things, which is the head, even Christ."—Ephesians 4:13, 15.

68

TREES DO NOT MAKE THE WIND

HAVE you ever wished, when in school and your teacher asked you questions, that you could, somehow, just press a button and your lips would automatically speak the right answers?

Of course we know that is impossible! We also know that words and deeds do not always make the truth and right. However our words and deeds tell what we think and what kind of person we are,—inside.

When I was a small boy I often thought that sometime I would attach a rope to the top of a tree and pull it back and forth and hope to make the wind blow, but I never got around to do it,—and it wouldn't have worked anyway, for trees do not make the wind blow.

The wind comes first and makes the trees bend and sway. It's God's way, working through nature, of pruning trees and forests. It's hard to explain where the wind comes from or how it starts but it is a part of God's way in nature.

Just saying a thing is right or just, does not make it so! Truth and Justice and Right come from God.

Sometimes we get mixed up in our heart and think wrong thoughts, and what happens? Out come a flock of bad words and, perhaps, untruths,—just as nature sometimes gets tangled up and causes a hurricane or a tornado,—and so a great deal of damage is done.

Trees sway because of the wind,—your words are spoken because of the kind of person you are inside.

Don't let your thoughts run wild. Keep close to God in prayer, and your words and deeds will come out all right.

"The wind bloweth where it will, you hear it but do not know whence it comes or whither it goes."—JOHN 3:8.

A PRAYER

FATHER, there is so much for which to be thankful that the little annoyances should not stand out so large in our thoughts. Keep us from being selfish in our prayers, and help us think of other people who need thy healing hand to rest upon them.

Bless little children in their play and protect them against harm due to carelessness. Keep them safe from serious illness and give them happiness.

Please accept our prayers in Jesus' name. Amen.

A MESSAGE FROM OUR BIBLE

"Jesus answered, Verily, verily, I say unto thee, Except a man be born of water and of the Spirit, he cannot enter into the Kingdom of God.

That which is born of flesh is flesh; and that which is born of the Spirit is spirit.

Marvel not that I said unto thee, Ye must be born again.

The wind bloweth where it listeth, and thou hearest the sound thereof, but canst not tell whence it cometh, and whither it goeth; so is every one that is born of the Spirit."—JOHN 3:5–8.

69

VACUUMS

A VACUUM receives nothing and gives nothing. It is a space where nothing is,—an empty space without even any air.

Now, all space dislikes being a vacuum,—it wants to be filled with something—even if it's only air.

Fill a small neck bottle with water and then turn it upside down. The water just does not seem to want to come out.

The next time your mother buys a can of consomme soup ask her to let you pour out the contents. Just punch a small hole in one edge of the top of the can and try emptying the soup into a saucepan. It gurgles and sputters and it just won't pour out easily.

Now punch another hole on the opposite edge of that can top and watch the liquid come pouring out very fast. As it comes out the lower hole, air rushes in the top hole and the can is perfectly satisfied. It's kept from being a vacuum, so it is glad to give up what it possesses.

After all, you and I are much like that. We like to possess things and we seem to take pride in having things that other people don't have! Perhaps we get a bit boastful at times when we have more of something than someone else. But after all, like consomme, things aren't much good sealed up inside. We can't play marbles with a boy who has no marbles!

Jesus was always going about doing good—giving whatever he had, to those in need. You would too, if you were filled with God's love.

You see, love and generosity coming into your heart makes you want to give out all the service you can muster to help others; and as you give to help others, more and more of God's spirit rushes in,—to keep you giving.

"Blessed are they that hunger and thirst after right-eousness; for they shall be filled."—MATTHEW 5 :6.

A PRAYER

DEAR God, fill our hearts with the love that Jesus had which made him so kind and thoughtful and unselfish. We are thy children, help us to understand how happiness is brought to us by giving and sharing.

Bless our homes, dear Lord, and grant that each of us will daily find ways by which we may show our love for one another.

Keep us ever worthy of thy trust in us and fill us with thy truth. Amen.

A MESSAGE FROM OUR BIBLE

"And seeing the multitude, he went up into a mountain; and when he was set, his disciples came unto him;

And he opened his mouth, and taught them, saying,

Blessed are the poor in spirit; for theirs is the kingdom of heaven.

Blessed are they that mourn; for they shall be comforted.

Blessed are the meek; for they shall inherit the earth.

Blessed are they which do hunger and thirst after righteousness; for they shall be filled.

Blessed are the merciful; for they shall obtain mercy.

Blessed are the pure in heart; for they shall see God.

Blessed are the peacemakers; for they shall be called the children of God.

Blessed are they which are persecuted for righteousness' sake; for theirs is the kingdom of heaven.

Blessed are ye, when men shall revile you, and persecute you, and say all manner of evil against you falsely, for my sake.

Rejoice and be exceeding glad; for great is your reward in heaven; for so persecuted they the prophets which were before you."—MATTHEW 5:1–12.

70

VALVES

WHEN you inflate your bicycle tire, of course, as you pump the air in, you expect it to stay there. You don't expect it to come right back out at you! Now the reason it does stay inside the tube is due to a little gadget called a valve which is automatically caused to close by the pressure of air on the inside, thus keeping the air from coming back out.

On every water system there is an open valve which lets the water run freely through pipes to the kitchen sink, or the fire protection hydrant beside the street.

When you want a drink of nice cold water you turn the faucet and open a valve. When there is a fire in your neighborhood someone turns in the alarm, the fire trucks come and firemen attach the hose to the nearby hydrant and open the valve and, sure enough, the hose fills and sends the water high to the roof tops and extinguishes the fire.

God gave Jesus to the world because He saw the fires of hate, greed and evil existing, and destroying people's lives. He brought love and joy into the world and was ready to give it to all.

But there were some who tried to shut Him out!

There are many today who close their hearts and minds to his teachings. They refuse to help keep the valves of the church open. To neglect the church and Sunday school tends to close the valves that stop the flow of Christianity.

The spirit of Jesus' teaching will protect and purify a city and make peace in the world—but you and I must keep the valves open and help carry Christ's message to all parts of the world.

"The wellsprings of wisdom are as a flowing brook."— PROVERBS 18 :4.

A PRAYER

HELP us, dear Lord, to hear thy voice as it comes to the world through thy Church. Teach us true loyalty that the truth of Christianity may spread throughout our community and into all the world through our efforts to keep thy love and purity alive as we go about our work and play.

We thank thee, O God, that thy love and loyalty were so strong in thy son Jesus that he never turned back from his great purpose of carrying thy gospel truth to all the world as he knew it.

He gave his life and service to thee and we are the richer spiritually and stronger because of his ever flowing spirit. Help us to keep that spirit of love and kindness and joy ever flowing into our homes and through us to others. Amen.

A MESSAGE FROM OUR BIBLE

"He that separateth himself seeketh his own desire,
And rageth against all sound wisdom.
A fool hath no delight in understanding,
But only that his heart may reveal itself.
The words of a man's mouth are as deep waters, and the wellspring of wisdom is as a flowing brook."—PROVERBS 18:1, 2, 4.

71

PURE, COLD WATER

AFTER you have played hard all the morning and you are hot and tired, and very hungry you rush into the kitchen,—and what is more wonderful and refreshing than a glass of pure cold water?

Of course, you know, that, when a person faints, a dash of cold water in her face will often revive her.

Some time ago I read of a new use of cold water. I recommend it highly! When you get angry with your brother or sister or your friend and you start sputtering at each other,—and your voices start rising higher and getting louder, each of you go at once and drink a full glass of pure, cold water. Then bathe your face with some pure, cold water. After you have done all this you will be ready to play together again,—your good nature completely restored.

On my farm in New Hampshire we have beautiful water. It has no taste, therefore, it is doubtless pure, and it is the coldest water I have ever used. The reason for this water being so pure and cold is because it comes from springs deep in God's good earth.

So it is with our friendships and our homes. If our friendship is on the surface and selfish, and we want our own way all the time, it isn't dependable and trustworthy—it's not satisfying. But, if, like the love of Jesus, our love is unselfish and comes from God—then it is pure and satisfying, and happiness and peace is the result. When things go wrong and problems arise, pray God to give you His strength to aid you.

"He leadeth me beside still waters. He restoreth my soul."—PSALM 23:2–3.

A PRAYER

WE THANK thee, our Father, for the depth of thy love. It is never failing. We thank thee for Jesus Christ who taught us how to find thee and in applying thy love, how to increase happiness and peace on the earth.

Grant that in thy strength we may apply ourselves to the wisdom that directs us to worship. Teach us to pray, that by this contact with thee, we may be committed to assurance of peace and love in the world.

Help us to avoid strife in petty things. Keep us above the discords and hatreds of lesser things and make us worthy of the highest, by the consecration of ourselves to thee, for our fellow men.

Grant that thy blessing may be felt by the young folks and give them a true sense of direction and security, through Jesus Christ our Lord. Amen.

A MESSAGE FROM OUR BIBLE

"The Lord is my shepherd; I shall not want.

He maketh me to lie down in green pastures; He leadeth me beside still waters.

He restoreth my soul; He leadeth me in the paths of righteousness for his name's sake.

Yea, though I walk through the valley of the shadow of death, I will fear no evil; for thou art with me; Thy rod and thy staff, they comfort me.

Thou preparest a table before me in the presence of mine enemies; Thou anointed my head with oil; My cup runneth over.

Surely goodness and mercy shall follow me all the days of my life; And I shall dwell in the house of the Lord for ever."—PSALM 23.

72

ONE KERNEL OF WHEAT

MANY years ago when I was a boy on our farm in Bath, New Hampshire, I used to help my father sow oats. We had no tractor or drills in those days so I carried a pail of oats and scattered the seeds over the fallow ground. I often wondered how many of those tiny seeds there were in my pail, and how many I let fly over the ten-acre field.

I never counted them, but not long ago I read somewhere that if one kernel of wheat is planted and if, in the fall, all the new kernels it produced, were in turn planted the next Spring, and so on, each year for sixteen years, there would be enough wheat to feed all the people in the whole world.

You have heard the story of the boy who wanted to give to missions. . . . His father said "I will give you one potato and enough land to plant it and its yield for the next five years." But he didn't count on its taking so many acres of his farm to plant the yield the fifth year!

Ask your Dad to give you a dime next month and two dimes the following month and so on for two years. I wonder what you will do with that half million dollars.

I hope you give it all to the missions of your church!

I'm sure you would like to see this whole world made Christian, wouldn't you? Wouldn't it be wonderful if you could trust everybody and know that all people were trying to be like Jesus?

That could happen in a very short few days if all the true Christians would win a non-Christian to Christ's way of living and each one of them in turn win someone else!

Easy isn't it. Let's all try it.

"I am ready to preach the gospel. . . ."—ROMANS 1:15.

A PRAYER

DEAR God, our Father, we thank thee for the beauty that is all around us. Help us to appreciate thy gifts—the sun, the sky, the clouds, the rain,—the very food we eat and the clear water we drink. Teach us not to complain, and forgive us when we do.

Above all we thank thee for thy expression of love, and grant that it may also be in our hearts to keep us happy and pleasant in our disposition at home and among our friends. Keep us faithful and trustworthy through the strength of Jesus. Amen.

A MESSAGE FROM OUR BIBLE

"So, as much as in me is, I am ready to preach the gospel to you that are at Rome also.

For I am not ashamed of the gospel of Christ; for it is the power of God unto salvation to every one that believeth; to the Jew first, and also to the Greek.

For therein is the righteousness of God revealed from faith to faith; as it is written, The just shall live by faith."—ROMANS 1:15–17.

73
WHEN A RACE HORSE WINS

I KNOW of very few things that are more beautiful than a trotting horse. He is so graceful and strong. So clear eyed and alive! He always brings tears of pure joy to my eyes as I see him trotting down the road.

It is a terrible pity, and, I think, so unchristian, to gamble on horse races.

As strange as it may seem, a horse never wins a race without a rider. A horse, to run or trot its best, always carries or pulls a load. That driver on the back of a beautiful horse, or in the sulky which the horse may be drawing, must be well-balanced with every ounce of his weight carefully arranged. More than that he must synchronize his every action and movement with the sway of the horse. Yes, he must even talk to his steed. In that way he builds up his confidence and the horse seems to reveal a new courage, and every muscle fairly quivers with eagerness to start.

The driver must, in reality, interlock himself with the horse he is driving,—he must almost be a part of him.

That race horse has no particular interest in crossing the finish line, but he seems to know he has his precious load to deliver safely ahead of any other.

I have noticed that a horse, free from harness, will stop to feed a lot by the side of the road, but when he is harnessed to a load he is eager to reach the top of the hill.

Who are the people you most admire and respect and look up to, and love? Are they not those who carry, for you, or for their church or community, the heaviest loads? Let us resolve to help them and to share their burdens even if it's only by an encouraging word. Jesus was always helping people win with their burdens.

"Bear one another's burdens and so fulfil the law of Christ."—GALATIANS 6:2.

A PRAYER

For the joy that has been ours this past year we are very grateful, dear Lord. Teach us to appreciate all the gifts that have come to us, and especially the gift of thy love.

We thank thee for Jesus who has meant so much to us all. Help us to follow his leadership in our work and school and home, and keep us loyal to thy church.

Grant that the children in other lands may be fed and clothed this coming year, and use us to carry thy message of pity and love into action. Amen.

A Message from Our Bible

"Bear ye one another's burdens, and so fulfil the law of Christ.

For if a man think himself to be something, when he is nothing, he deceiveth himself.

But let every man prove his own work, and then shall he have rejoicing in himself alone, and not in another.

For every man shall bear his own burden.

Let him that is taught in the word communicate unto him that teacheth in all good things."—GALATIANS 6: 2–6.

74

WHISTLES

In one of the cities in which I have lived, I recall that some distance from the Parsonage there was a railroad track, and every morning at about 5:45 a train would come steaming over the tracks, and as it approached a crossing it let forth with a very loud whistle—four blasts. I knew one of the engineers and informed him that he awakened me—and others—much too early each day! After that he would reduce the whistle to four short toots!

The whistle had to be blown because, sometime, a life might be saved thereby.

I once saw a person very nearly killed by a freight train,—she wanted to be hit! How the whistle blew! However, she remained on the track, but finally the train was able to stop within a foot or two from her.

You see, a whistle can't save a person's life unless he wants to be saved. Unless he heeds the warning! I used to like to go out in front of our house in New Hampshire and "skid" down the steep embankment to the railroad tracks. A long trestle crossed the Ammonoosuc River and once in a while I would dare cross over that high bridge on the open ties. But I'd be very careful to first listen for the whistle of an approaching train.

I used to like to take my shotgun and go out in the fields and hunt woodchucks. Quite often, before I would see one, I would hear a whistle and then I would go home. When a woodchuck whistles—he, and all the others within hearing, rush into their holes to safety.

Your fathers and mothers often warn you against doing something. So do your teachers or your friends. It's up to you to heed all warnings, for only you can keep yourselves from the dangers of bad habits and wrong doing.

"I did not cease to warn everyone."—Acts 20:31.

A PRAYER

Our Father, whose spirit lives in our hearts, guide us in the way of truth and honesty. Help us to know what is right and so, to shun the wrong.

Give us clear vision that we may see the needs of others, especially of the many children who lack the necessary things of life.

Make us dependable and trustworthy and give us strength to meet every obligation, and every opportunity that comes before us. Help us to realize that thy love may be expressed through us, and may we so live as to show forth the generosity which was in Jesus as He went about doing good. Give us faith that we may trust one another and help us to be trustworthy ourselves. In Jesus' name. Amen.

A Message from Our Bible

"Therefore watch and remember, that I ceased not to warn every one night and day with tears.

I have coveted no man's silver, or gold, or apparel.

I have showed you all things, how that so laboring ye ought to support the weak, and to remember the words of the Lord Jesus, how he said, It is more blessed to give than to receive.

And when he had thus spoken, he kneeled down, and prayed with them all."—Acts 20:31, 33, 35–36.

75

WINDOW PANES

WINDOWS, of course, are put into houses so that daylight can come in, and also, to furnish an opportunity for fresh air to be let in upon occasion. How bright and cheery houses look that have these picture windows in them, as compared with small ones or even windows with small panes of glass.

Now, one important service that windows give, of course, is to allow a person to see what is going on outside.

One rather cold winter day I watched a child standing very close to the window. She was watching some children and several dogs running around outside in the snow, in a neighbor's yard, and as she looked so eagerly, I noticed she shifted from one pane of glass to another in the window. I wondered why and stepped over to find out. It being a cold day, and as she stood very close to the window pane, her breath caused vapor to form and freeze on the glass. This, of course, obstructed her view and so she moved over to a clear pane, and pretty soon that one fogged up, and again she moved to another.

I wonder if you have ever come home from school and vow to your mother that you will "never speak to" a certain girl again. Of course, you don't mean it—and the very next day you are both friends once more. Why do you seem to dislike someone for a little while? Perhaps it's your fault. Possibly you just won't look for the good points in that person. Try and change your point of view. Don't look through the fog of your own selfishness—move over to another pane that's clear and bright and see the good in that little friend.

God wants you to see clearly with a Christ-like mind.

"Now we see through a glass, darkly; but then face to face. . . ."—I CORINTHIANS 13:12.

A PRAYER

Jesus, our Lord, we thank thee for the Church to which we go and offer up our adoration and praise in worship to our Father in Heaven. Thou hast set aside a day of calmness for our body, mind and soul, and our thoughts and actions are trained on thee and thy love.

As parents and leaders of youth are consecrated to lead young minds toward thee, give them strength and inspiration to live as thou hast taught. Bless those who are ill, whose bodies are in pain. Help the children who are crippled in any way.

Inspire the people with influence to see clearly the way to peace on earth and to good will and love among nations. Let there be no more wars. Give us a will to learn of thy love and to follow in its way as taught and lived by Jesus, our Saviour. Amen.

A Message from Our Bible

"When I was a child, I spake as a child, I understood as a child, I thought as a child; but when I became a man, I put away childish things.

For now we see through a glass darkly; but then face to face; now I know in part; but then shall I know even as also I am known.

And now abideth faith, hope, charity, these three; but the greatest of these is charity."—I CORINTHIANS 13: 11–13.

76

STAINED GLASS WINDOWS

When you break a pane of glass in the kitchen window at home with a baseball, your Dad just goes to the store and buys another. But with stained glass windows such as are seen in many churches, it isn't that easy. Every window is hand-made and designed like a picture puzzle. Each tiny piece must be shaped and cemented in its proper place, and in such a way that the colors will blend so as to be harmonious with the whole.

Most important of all is the light that shines through or upon the windows, for "light is the glory of the stained glass windows—by it they come alive" and reveal their beauty.

Have you seen those streamers that glisten in the sun as they wave in front of gasoline stations? Light strikes them in such a way to make them fairly sparkle!

A diamond ring is most radiant to the eye when seen under a light.

People are much like that—especially children—they wake up in the morning and if it's raining they often grumble because they can't play ball or go to the country for the weekend. And then the sun comes out and all is bright and happy.

But real happiness doesn't depend upon sunlight, but upon God's light shining through your heart causing other people to love you—and causing them to be happy because of you.

So I hope you will arrange your life with the idea of making others happy because they see in you, and working through you, God's light.

"Let your light so shine before men that they may see your good works and glorify your Father which is in Heaven."—MATTHEW 5:16.

A PRAYER

Dear Lord, teach us to be kind to those children who do not have a happy home. Give us many opportunities to befriend them that they may see more clearly the Christian way of life. Help them see the truth through us, and so keep us from doing wrong or speaking thoughtlessly, lest our example leads them astray.

Grant that we may keep thee before us and may thy light shine into our hearts that we may give joy to others as we express the love of Jesus. Amen.

A Message from Our Bible

"Ye are the light of the world. A city that is set on a hill cannot be hid.

Neither do men light a candle, and put it under a bushel, but on a candlestick; and it giveth light unto all that are in the house.

Let your light so shine before men, that they may see your good works, and glorify your Father which is in heaven."—Matthew 5:14–16.

77

WISHBONES

THANKSGIVING DAY is a time of great rejoicing in most all of our American homes. It means a lot to eat, and usually at grandma's home!

At the end of the meal someone is sure to pipe up and say: "Who has the wishbone?"

That wishbone is very important to the person who has it. He puts it near the stove so it will get good and dry and brittle then he chooses a partner and each takes hold of one prong and they pull until it breaks, and the one who holds the longest end is the winner and, of course, is supposed to have his wish come true.

Did you ever stop to realize, as you were pulling on those prongs, that there was no meat on the wishbone?

There is no "meat" on just wishes either? Do you ever wish you might have all "A"s on your report card? Wishes won't do it. It takes good hard work. When you are given home work you must spend quite a bit of time on your lessons. Not wishes but work will bring results.

Wishes won't make you happy. If you want to be happy you must do the things that make for happiness. Of course, you wish every child in Korea would have enough to eat but many of those children will die of starvation unless you help feed them. Wishes won't do it. It takes food.

So while we eat heartily of our Thanksgiving Dinner let us pray and resolve to put aside a dime or a dollar each week, and give to the missions of the church.

You recall that little jingle—"If wishes were horses beggars would ride." But wishes are not horses or automobiles so most of us must walk and work. Let us not be satisfied with just wishing.

"He who has two coats, let him share . . . and he who has food . . . likewise."—LUKE 3:11.

A PRAYER

Our Father who art in heaven, we look to thee for help when things go wrong. We ask for many favors which often we do not deserve, and should not have.

Help us leave the answer in thy hands and be content, for thy wisdom is far greater than ours.

As we pray for happiness, guide us into ways of service that makes for happiness right around us. When we pray to have more friends, help us to be more friendly. We pray earnestly that thy love may be spread out into all the world, so make us more loving and thoughtful, and cause our wishes to become active within us. Amen.

A Message from Our Bible

"And now also the axe is laid unto the root of the trees; every tree therefore which bringeth not forth good fruit is hewn down, and cast into the fire.

And the people asked him, saying, What shall we do then?

He answereth and saith unto them, He that hath two coats, let him impart to him that hath none; and he that hath meat, let him do likewise."—Luke 3:9–11.